ORGANIZATIONAL LEARNING
AND COMMUNITIES OF PRACTICE
IN A HIGH-TECH MANUFACTURING FIRM

ORGANIZATIONAL LEARNING
AND COMMUNITIES OF PRACTICE
IN A HIGH-TECH MANUFACTURING FIRM

Anthony M. Barrett

The Edwin Mellen Press
Lewiston•Queenston•Lampeter

Library of Congress Cataloging-in-Publication Data

Barrett, Anthony M.
  Organizational learning and communities of practice in a high-tech manufacturing
firm / by Anthony M. Barrett.
    p. cm.
  Includes bibliographical references and index.
  ISBN 0-7734-5902-2
    1. Organizational learning. 2. Social learning. I. Title.

  HD58.82.B36 2006
  658.3'124--dc22

                                                                    2006041891

hors série.

A CIP catalog record for this book is available from the British Library.

The Edwin Mellen Press
Box 450
Lewiston, New York
USA 14092-0450

The Edwin Mellen Press
Box 67
Queenston, Ontario
CANADA L0S 1L0

The Edwin Mellen Press, Ltd.
Lampeter, Ceredigion, Wales
UNITED KINGDOM SA48 8LT

Printed in the United States of America

Table of Contents

Research Design: Research context; the organizational context;
qualitative research; data generation procedures; ethnic considerations;
ethnographic validity; researcher as instrument; delimitations and
limitations.

Patterns in the Literature: the Pattern Making Shop; learning; multiple
perspectives of organization studies; historical patterns and seminal
thinkers; communities of practice; social learning theory.

Data Analysis: The foundry context; coding; emergent and salient
themes; social learning revisited; organizational metaphors.

Foreword

The birth of a theory: innovation at the boundaries

When Anthony asked me to write a foreword for his book, I had a number of options. I could praise him for outlining a history of learning theory as a story of ideas that focuses on actors who were carrying these ideas forward in various ways. I could congratulate him for taking the framework of social learning theory into a manufacturing context and exploring with wit and insight what learning meant to various groups. I could mention the way in which he used the production process at the site of his fieldwork as a metaphor for organizing his analysis.

All this would be true. But you can find it all out by reading the book.

I thought the most useful thing I could do is to add some personal touch to his history of learning theory by telling my side of the story of how the concept of communities of practice was born. Anthony is already taking a personal approach to the history of ideas so adding a personal perspective would be in line with his writing. This is the early story as I remember it, told from my perspective. Other participants surely have their own versions. But this is the nature of stories: They represent the lived experience of protagonists and therefore have more than one face.

There are also intellectual reasons for telling this story. It illustrates some of the very processes the resulting theory is meant to account for—practices, communities, boundaries, and identities. And as a result, underlying this story is the outline of a theory of innovation based on communities of practice.

As Anthony notes, the Institute for Research on Learning was started by the Xerox foundation in response to the 1983 "A Nation at Risk" report of the US

Department of Education. John Seely Brown, head of the Xerox Palo Alto Research Center at the time, convinced then Xerox CEO David Kearns, who had publicly complained about US education, of the need for some fundamental research. Schools of education would focus on educational techniques, but it was also necessary to reconsider more fundamental assumptions about learning. In particular it was important to look at the wide variety of ways people learn successfully in daily life. The charter of the institute was to "rethink learning."

Learning at the time was mostly the bailiwick of disciplines like psychology and artificial intelligence. But rethinking learning required a broader mix of perspectives. The institute brought together scholars from a variety of disciplines, including psychology, education, and computer science, but also anthropology, linguistics, literary criticism, physics, and mathematics. We had fights. It never came to fists, but sparks did fly. The question of what is learning quickly came down to assumptions various disciplines were making about what a learner is and what might qualify as a meaningful account of something like human learning.

Imagine the following conversation between a computer scientist and an anthropologist:

Your little book about your island and your tribes, it is good literature, but it is not science. You are just describing things, you do not provide any explanatory mechanisms about what is happening.

It is always hard to be told that what one does is not science in an academic context where science is revered. The anthropologist would then turn back and say something like:

But your little program, you know, that models how kids learn subtraction, maybe you think you are really explaining a phenomenon because you can reproduce some observable data, but in fact, you have a model of learning in which there is no learner. There is nobody doing the learning.

The concept of community of practice arose as a unit of analysis of learning in which we could find explanatory mechanisms, while placing at the core of our concerns the learner as a social being in the process of becoming. It enabled us to analyze learning as the negotiation of meaning as well as the acquisition of skills.

The story illustrates some key ingredients for innovation from a communities of practice perspective. The first one was the importance of boundaries. All communities of practice create boundaries, unavoidably, because joint learning creates a distinction between those who have participated in it and those who have not. Our disciplinary fights were boundary encounters among practices. At these boundaries, perspectives are dislocated and the competence one has developed in one's community does not function properly. Assumptions have to be reconsidered. This is what makes boundary encounters valuable learning opportunities – a potential source of radical innovation.

The second ingredient was the focus on a significant issue such as learning. The enterprise of rethinking learning was one we all believed in and cared about. Our shared commitment to it enabled us to keep engaging across disciplinary boundaries. One cannot overstate the importance of this joint enterprise—and the institute's commitment to it—as a container for the process. It was often quite uncomfortable and sometimes even painful. But only sustained engagement would allow us to create the necessary field for innovation.

Thirdly, the scholars who came together were steeped in their disciplines. Their identities were invested in their disciplines. They were successful scholars with deep expertise, not dilettantes leisurely exploring the landscape. Their commitment to their disciplines made for sparks. It brought about serious confrontations of ideas with a productive intensity that was unlikely to be resolved by a simple retreat into any discipline. In addition, these committed scholars steeped in their disciplines brought another important ingredient: the ability to recognize when something new came up that was worth paying attention to, something that their discipline would not consider old hat.

And finally, there were the young ones, people like me, who were not yet really committed to any discipline yet. We had an open identity and could embrace the boundary as a place to be. We did not have the judgment and the depth of our elders. We were apprentices. Each of us had a mentoring connection to someone. During this time I was primarily an apprentice of Jean Lave, the anthropologist with whom I co-authored the initial book on communities of practice. But beyond these individual relationships, we were mostly apprentices of this boundary encounter. These conceptual fights were the best intellectual schooling one could ever dream of. Everybody was transformed, elders and apprentices alike. But for us apprentices, this became a crucial formative experience. The boundary encounter became our practice.

Then the institute went on to function as a research institute. The fights gave way to more focused research projects. Still many of us kept working on the early questions. I certainly did. Today, the institute does not exist as such. But for me its early burst of innovation remains the core of my inquiry. It lives on in everything I do.

And now it lives on even further as I find myself invited to write a foreword for the work of a new generation ...

Etienne Wenger

Etienne Wenger earned his Ph.D. in Computer Science from the University of California at Irvine. He is a renowned expert and consultant on knowledge management and communities of practice.

Preface

This research project used an ethnographic study as a backdrop to address theoretical and philosophical concepts related to organizational learning and social learning theory. Current social learning theory (Wenger, 1998) suggests that learning contributes to the formation of a person's identity during social participation. Contrary to the notion that learning is mainly a transfer of information between individuals, learning is viewed as an interdependent social enterprise in which the situation informs the lessons learned and thereby informs the identity of the learner. The context of this study was a custom machine shop that produces molds for packaging and bicycle helmets.

To frame the rationale for this research, the ramifications of modern, interpretative, and postmodern traditions of organizational studies were considered. An interpretative approach was selected; however, multiple perspectives were considered to add depth and perspective to the units of analysis. There were two guiding and interrelated research questions: What is the organizational culture of this firm? How does this firm learn? In light of social learning theory, both questions are inextricably linked.

Two movements were considered to explore this culture- learning connection. Organizational learning attempts to foster collective learning and may be analyzed from three perspectives within an organizational context: normative, developmental, and capability (DiBella & Nevis, 1998). Communities of practice, seeing learning as participation in a social practice, which in turn forms the identity of the participants, fits within the latter perspective.

The findings encountered in this study were subtle yet applicable to understanding learning in the work place. For instance, some class distinction, particularly about learning was evident and added stress and competition that hindered social participation and suggested that learning was less than optimal. The disconnect between the organization's espoused values and active values frustrated some employees as did not making use of all employees' energies and capabilities. If left unaddressed these intangible social particulars will continue to erode the positive regard between employees and toward the firm, thereby hampering productivity. In essence, social learning theory indicates an unintended curriculum informs the social situation, in this context the workplace, commandeering the planned lesson.

Another way to put this axiom is that humans can not not learn. Humans learn to adapt and cope with life's perplexities and, unless attention is paid to what they actually are learning, intended and unintended lessons can work at cross purposes. Minding the social climate is as important as the planned lessons. There is an organic quality to this social dimension of learning in which the stress needs to be placed on learning as opposed to training. The emphasis needs to be on the whole person embedded in the social context and encompassing their life experience and knowledge. The clout of social learning theory is found in social dimension of the situation, the relationships, and the distribution of knowledge. The individual agency of each learner plays a supporting role as opposed to a staring role in social learning theory.

Social learning theory and this research suggest those participants whose identity has been shaped by the practice are more likely to be the most capable and effective employees. With full participation and engagement in a community of practice, participants' knowledge becomes embedded with the community, takes root, and grows to fruition. The social character of knowledge and human life is seminal to understanding how an organization learns.

Acknowledgements

First, I would like to acknowledge and thank the nine men at Delta Technologies, including the owner, who gave their personal time for interviews. Many others at Delta Technologies welcomed me into their communities of practice and shared their thoughts in the lunchroom when they were on breaks or over a workbench while they stayed on task. Their candid remarks and willingness to share their stories and points of view was the essential core of this study. The rich data they provided, I believe, points to the importance of the social dimensions of learning. Without their generosity and candor, this study would have been impossible.

Next, I would like to thank the many professors and other professionals at the University of Idaho who encouraged me with their friendship, generosity, and kindness during my years as an employee and student. This list begins with the members of my committee: Drs. Martha Yopp, James Gregson, Nick Sanyal, and Jeff Bailey. Other professors who enriched my experiences as a student and as a human being are Stephen and Anna Banks, Nancie Burns-McCoy, Dave Christian, David Croasdell, Joy Passanante, Molly Stock, George Wray, and Mike Whiteman. Colleagues at Information Technologies Services (ITS), Rich and Marsha Benson, Daryl Power, and Anita Mackey welcomed me into their community of practice in telecommunications. A special thanks goes to Tony Pishl at ITS who helped rescued my hard drive at an critical point of my writing process. Other colleagues who helped me with technical issues were John Snakenberg, Allen Kitchel, Jared Merrick, and George Porter. Thanks also to Jim Cassetto for office space and a computer during my last year. Fellow students with whom I grateful to have share my academic journey with are: Ashley Ater-

Kranov, Simba and Koi Tirima, Nancy Deringer, Michèle D'Arcy-Evans and Maarten de Laat. Brian Fast and Jeremy Giddens two long time friends who earned their doctorates before me also encouraged me during tough times,.

I also am grateful to Gleanne Wray and Jeannie Anderson for their critically constructive comments on my earlier drafts. Thanks also to Candace Chenoweth for her editing skills for this book.

I feel extremely fortunate to have Etienne Wenger and John Smith as friends and am grateful for their gracious invitation to join them in the online foundations workshop, then CPSquare (an online community of practice of communities of practice), and the conference in Santa Cruz. I feel blessed to know them and to be in touch with them as learning partners. Their personal encouragement and thoughtful posts have been an inspiration. Also, Tony DiBella, Terri Deems, and Mary Crossan in the field of organizational learning encouraged me along the way toward the completion this project. It has meant so much to get numerous e-mails of encouragement from them and to feel their acceptance as a colleague.

Last and certainly not least, I am profoundly grateful to my family. My daughter Maya, whose smile I carried with me, has been so patient with her father for not spending more time with her during this project. I am also especially grateful to my partner and spouse Mary Furnari, for her profoundly evident love and encouragement to see me through this endeavor. We both laughed out loud when I read to her what Etienne Wenger wrote in an acknowledgement to his family " ...that I am not quite sure whether to thank them or to apologize to them." (Wenger, 1998, p. xv) As is so often the case, Etienne elegantly describes the complexity and contradictions this life-world. In acknowledging the joys and struggles I have shared with family and friends, I am reminded how easily I assume and take for granted those invisible ties of the social world. This study has taught me how influential and significant those social ties are in how we learn and who we become as human beings.

Dedication

This book is dedicated posthumously to my father, Marvin R. Barrett, who worked remarkably hard to support his family and knew more than he could ever say.

CHAPTER ONE

Research Design

Our vision is more obstructed by what we think we know than by our lack of
knowledge.   Stendahl, 1976, p. 7

Introduction

This chapter and each subsequent chapter will begin with a depiction of
the work process and context of a custom mold shop. Without a brief summary of
these processes and details, the work accomplished by this firm is hard to discern.
Reflecting on the firm's organizational processes, I have chosen to format this
research project so that its chapters resonate with the production process of this
custom mold shop. Thus, I have renamed and reordered the traditional research
format to better represent the organization I studied and to enhance the
explanation of its organizational dynamics. A "thick description" (Geertz, 1973)
of the context is essential to qualitative research, and such a description includes
an interpretative characteristic of the context (Schwandt, 2001). Therefore, this
first section will describe and interpret the community and region. In addition to
the context of the organization being interpreted, the first step in creating an
aluminum cast mold, the design phase, will be briefly described.

Research Context

Nestled in the rolling hills of the rural inland Pacific Northwest of the United
States, Delta Technologies[1] was started in a garage in approximately 1987. As

---

[1] The name of this firm is fictitious and pseudonyms are used to protect confidentiality.

sculptor and visual artist respectively, Rick and Linda were introduced to casting molten metals while pursing their Master of Fine Arts degrees at a nearby university. Having moved from the Mid-West, they liked the area and decided to stay after graduation. The nearest town to Delta Technologies is only two miles away, and it has been depressed economically since several lumber mill closings during previous years. This town had focused its energies and loyalties on the logging industry, so much so that the high school mascot's name is timber related. Even with several colleges and universities within a 50-mile radius, the school district's test scores have the lowest rating in a state that is low to begin with. Residents have related stories that high school students have been known to graduate although functionally illiterate. The rationale is that since they would be working in the mill or logging in the forest, it would not matter if they could read. ("Tom," personal communication, Oct. 20, 2001).

The challenge of running a company that requires technical expertise in a community where education is considered optional is a formidable challenge. On the other hand, the local universities provide fresh, bright engineering students, with little experience, but who are eager to apply what they have studied: designing and building things. These new engineering students balance out the labor pool of locals who are seeking a job merely to put food on the table rather than as a professional career. The ingredients of tension between the "college boys" and the "good ol' boys" are just below the surface. This tension comes to the surface only when speaking separately with the employees; I observed good-natured humor and camaraderie on the shop floor until I started interviewing.

The devices Delta Technologies produces are custom-made aluminum cast molds to form particle foam for protective packaging, many of which are used for computer-related components. They also include molds for producing foam for bike helmets manufactures of these helmets have forwarded letters have been forwarded from helmet manufactures from people who survived bike accidents and are alive because of the helmets; the workers proudly mentioned these letters to me. Some mold tools are small enough to hold in one hand others comprise sets of molds on a rack as large as a king-sized bed that must be moved with a forklift. The going rate for these "tools" ranges from $10,000 to $100,000, and they can be produced in a matter of weeks. Delta Technologies' customer list includes firms such as Hewlett-Packard, Apple Computer, and Bell Helmets. In 1999 it was reported that Delta Technologies grossed approximately $3.5 million and that the company had grown from 15 to over 60 employees. State officials, including university presidents and the state governor, hailed Delta Technologies as a model for rural development in the state.

The manufacturing process for these molds begins in the design shop. Measurements and shapes must be precise, or the entire tool must be remanufactured at Delta Technologies' expense. Delta Technologies has a reputation for tools that cost more; however, Delta Technologies stands by their product and its quality. These tools must endure high steam pressure and extreme heat changes. On more than one occasion, I saw and heard of tools being returned for repair or because specifications were outside the tolerance that customer had ordered. The curves and corners of each mold have some "room to wiggle," but if the size of the mold is off too much, corrections must be made. These problems eat into the profits since Delta Technologies must pay for roundtrip shipping, as well as for the time and materials to fix the problems.

Intrinsically related to the design shop is the sales department, which also could be called customer relations and service. The sales representative is the contact person who conveys the project's specifications to a project manager and the design shop. The sales representative also negotiates the price and deadline for completion of the project with the customer. This negotiation can last days or just a few moments, depending on how long it takes to develop an estimate for each stage of production. An hourly estimate is given and recorded, then compared to actual time spent. The sales representative and a designated project manager work closely to insure that specifications are maintained throughout the production process. Being a sales representative is one of the more stressful roles at Delta

Technologies. The sales representative must balance selling the company's ability to produce molds yet with trusting that others will make thousands of decisions correctly. As problems arise, as with any complex project, the sales representative must stay in contact with and diplomatically explain glitches to customers. For example, one sales representative recalled knowing the home phone number, as well as the name of the customer's wife, because he had kept in such close contact over the production time span. Sales representatives also devise cost and deadline estimates, which become agreements. With all the details that go into mold making, attention to technicalities is essential.

Stress for the project managers is not far behind. Project managers must negotiate the workflow within each department and oversee that both project specifications and deadlines are kept. For customers such as Apple Computer or Hewlett-Packard, deadlines are crucial since products cannot be shipped until the molds are completed and packaging foam is made to protect their components. Each mold project starts in the design shop, where the pressure to be accurate and on time is intense.

Placed between the front office and the shop floor is the design shop. The approximate size of the room is a 12' x 25' rectangle. Windows look out to the shop on one side and into the cubicles of the front office on the other side. The design shop is quiet compared to the shop floor, except when the door from the shop is opened. There are four computer workstations with 21" computer monitors. At one end is a room that holds the server that networks the entire company. Next to the server room is a room that holds a large instrument that takes extremely precise measurements of three-dimensional objects, such as bike helmets, and transfers those measurements into mathematical data that can be uploaded into engineering software such as Velum ®. Looking something like an X-ray machine in a hospital, along with the software program, this instrument allows designs to be retained and sizes and measurement to be adjusted.

On the other side of the room is a white project board with a grid that takes up nearly the entire wall. Projects are tracked here, with the project name on the vertical axis and the days in production on a horizontal axis along the top. From this board, specific people are assigned work to accomplish. The board serves as reference point, and nearly everyone involved in production can be seen checking a project's status from time to time, similar to a central clock in medieval city.

A daily production meeting takes place in the design shop. This meeting consists of approximately twenty-five people (mostly males) who crowd into the room. The exchange of information is subtle; voices are low, and if one is not listening carefully it is easy to miss the exchange of information. The status of each project is reported as the production manager names each project. Three codes designate the project's status: 1) green means on time and budget; 2) yellow indicates some concerns, but just slightly over time and budget; 3) red indicates over budget and late. The status of each project is recorded and adjustments are made to the project board. Thus, a report may be categorized as: "It's yellow in the pattern shop." The production meetings can last ten minutes or go on longer, depending on what issues come up. During the meeting important issues related to production are discussed or announced. Managers from the front office slip in to listen or make announcements. There is also an all-shop meeting once a month, but daily concerns are addressed primarily at the production meeting.

Once the production meeting ends, the design shop quiets down and people discuss details of projects in front of the project board. Several employees work at a computer together in an apprenticeship situation, discussing the finer points of a design software program called Velum ®. General suggestions surface, such as the advice to "only change a little bit at a time because if you have to go back, there is less to replace." Velum ®, similar to CAD but more user-friendly, is a complex program that takes years to master. A strong understanding of geometry is needed to make full use of this three-dimensional design program. As the object on the monitor is rotated, the person in the learner role exclaims, "I love this stuff!"

Everyone who works at Delta Technologies seems to enjoy their work. The general tone I sensed in the work place at can be paradoxically characterized as a "relaxed intensity." People were focused on the task at hand, but they were also easy-going. In the Staff Handbook, the final guiding value is a commitment to humor. That commitment to humor is present and balances out the focused intensity and stress to get products out the door.

Part of the intensity in the design shop stems from the need to get a project design completed in order for production to start; part from the need for thousands of measurements and details to be within a customer's range of tolerance. Attention to detail and good decision making is stressed everywhere at Delta Technologies, especially in the first step of the production process. Part of the complexity of designing a mold stems from the shifting back and forth between a positive object and the exact negative. Molds are the opposite of what is being produced. Letters or numbers must be reversed and transposed. Every curve or angle must be checked and rechecked for the design to be correct. One must think in geometric dimensions to get a sense of the issues and complexities of these objects. As I listened in on conversations using the specialized terminology, I understood perhaps 25% of the discussion. Seasoned employees with more than five years of experience told me they understand about 60% of mold-making dynamics. Only a handful of employees consider themselves fluent in understanding a project in all its detail and complexity, from design to completion. The challenge for Delta Technologies is to expand the number of people who are able to make knowledgeable decisions to produce quality molds. In other words, learning needs to occur between knowledgeable, experienced employees and those with less or no experience.

The following pages will describe and explore the context in which learning takes place, how learning presently occurs, and what appears to work best to enhance learning.

Interest in Organizational Learning

My initial interest in organizational learning emerged as I attempted to make sense of a stressful and chaotic experience as a middle-level manager at a university. I was seeking practical answers to endemic organizational and personnel problems within the unit I managed. Prior to the management position at this university, I taught in the public schools of inner city Los Angeles County while completing my master's degree. Thus, with the combination of management experience and my longstanding interest in education and learning, I reasoned that learning was part of a long-term solution to organizational dysfunction.

Moreover, the broader context of the early 1990s insinuated that information technology and personal computers were the harbingers of a coming revolution. Information processed becomes knowledge, and knowledge can be managed toward more effective organizations, and knowledge can be managed to give a competitive advantage (Stata, 1989). Those who had knowledge processing skills and who could build on those skills by learning more became more valuable. Drucker (1999) affirms that the information revolution has produced and empowered "the knowledge worker." Drucker (1999) concludes his argument by suggesting that the knowledge worker increase in power extends beyond salary demands. "Bribing the knowledge worker on whom these industries depend will therefore simply not work... It will have to be done by turning them from subordinates into fellow executives, and from employees, however well paid, into partners" (p. 57).

Ironically, the public sector is one place where, hypothetically, workers are the owners. Yet, in my experience, many employees at the university where I worked were concerned more with petty turf battles than with their unit functioning more effectively. Through the "school of hard knocks," I came to realize that organizational learning was not simply about teaching self-evident principles. Acknowledging my blind spot(s) led me to be wary of quick fixes or "flavor-of-the-month" management fads (e.g., Brindle & Stearns, 2001; Coles, 1999). Each organization is unique, much like a family, with its history, special dynamics and context.

For instance, family therapist Mary Pipher (1996 p. 28) argues that "theories are limited by time and place." Theories emerge from certain particulars that were present. When those particulars change or disappear, context-bound theories are drained of relevance. Theory is like a cognitive map of salient features of a field. However, as a field or city changes, the map must be revised or redrawn. Or as Pipher put it, "Certain kinds of therapy made sense [at one time]. But psychological theories have a short shelf-life. Our old ideas about how to help are useless in the face of new realities. We attempt to solve problems with theories developed for a world that no longer exists" (p. 29).

Similarly, the time and motion studies of Fredrick W. Taylor (1856-1915), as well as his scientific management theory, are no longer apt in knowledge-laden high-tech firms. Scientific management was developed in the midst of an industrial revolution when steam engines were in full use and the internal combustion engine had only been recently invented. Today, for instance, in one second, 44 gigabytes of data (approximately 40 complete sets of encyclopedias) can be transferred through a piece of fiber optic cable as thick as a human hair to another time zone at the speed of light. Hydrogen fuel cells will likely replace the internal combustion engine in the next generation. We are entering the time of which sociologist Daniel Bell (1973) wrote in The Coming of Post-Industrial Society (see Hatch, 1997, p. 25 for a summary). In this society, Bell argues, change will be the only constant (also see Schön, 1973). In light of the rapid change and concomitant short shelf life of theories, it is my contention that we are served best by a multiple perspective approach for theoretical grounding, such as is found in Organization Theory (Hatch, 1997).

Since I argue that theories have inherent limitations, their values can be adjudicated by the usefulness of their powers of explanation (interpretations) and by how they may enhance human existence. Thus, philosophically, I find resonance in the broad paradigm of pragmatism. The ideas of John Dewey (1859-1952), Thomas Kuhn (1970), Richard Rorty (1979), and Cornel West (1989) ring true to me in their lucid interpretations of philosophical "problems" and their aspirations of enhancing human dignity.

Like any philosophical paradigm, pragmatism has its limitations; I have chosen to study the thinkers mentioned above. It has simply come down to what makes the most sense in light of my values. It is my genuine aspiration to see organizations enhanced so that human potential can be realized more fully. After all, "adults today spend more of their time and energy engaged in work than in any other wakeful activity" (Deems, 1997, p. 16, citing Armon, 1993). It is the goal of this research to see how an organization learns and thereby enhance the health and learning capacity of that organization.

Qualitative Research

A qualitative research methodology was selected for this research project because of my background in cultural anthropology and my philosophical convictions that organizations are best understood situated in their natural context. The cultural anthropology rationale will be discussed in the section titled "Researcher as Instrument." Philosophically, a qualitative research methodology was selected since "the nature of the social phenomena to be explored" (Morgan & Smircich, 1980, p. 491) is an organization in all its complexity and ambiguity.

It is my position that there is a place for traditional quantitative research methodologies in organizational studies. In fact, during my interviews I used an Organizational Learning Profile (DiBella & Nevis, 1998, p. 100) to elicit topics of discussion that would facilitate organizational learning, along with the purpose of generating data. In some interviews, the profile provoked thoughtful reflection; at other times, there was confusion over interpretations of meanings in the profile. I used definitions from DiBella and Nevis (1998) so my explanations would be equivalent with each interview, yet I noticed some ambiguity with how each informant interpreted the instrument. Thus, the use of this profile gave me a new appreciation of the limits of a textual instrument or questionnaires since all requires interpretation by the respondents. In the end, the Organizational Learning Profile played a minor role in the research methodology and will be discussed in detail in Chapter Three.

The research methodology selected for this study is qualitative, with the understanding that any definition of such a historically complex topic does not suit all parties or situations. Denzin & Lincoln (1994, p. 2) offer a generic definition that fits well for this project:

> Qualitative research is multimethod in focus, involving an interpretative, naturalistic approach to its subject matter. This means that qualitative researchers study things in their natural settings, attempting to make sense of, or interpret, phenomena in terms of the meaning people bring to them. Qualitative research involves the studied use and collection of a variety of empirical materials – case study, personal experience, introspection, life story, interview, observational, historical, interactional, and visual text— that describe routine and problematic moments and meanings in individuals' lives. Accordingly, qualitative researchers deploy a wide range of interconnected methods, hoping always to get a better fix on the subject matter at hand.

The wide range of interconnected methods used to understand learning at Delta Technologies included participant observation, interviews using both non-structured and semi-structured formats, videotaped events, and document analysis. Thus, among the several traditions under the qualitative research rubric, the tradition that fit best the research question I was asking was an ethnographic approach. Atkinson and Hammersley (1994, p. 248) describe ethnographic research methodology as follows:

- A strong emphasis on exploring the nature of particular social phenomena, rather than setting out to test hypotheses about them.

- A tendency to work primarily with "unstructured" data, that is, data that have not been coded at the point of data collection in terms of closed sets of analytic categories.

- [The] investigation of a small number of cases, perhaps just one case, in detail.

- Analysis of data that involves explicit interpretation of meanings and functions of human actions, the product of which mainly takes the form of verbal descriptions and explanation with quantification and statistical analysis playing a subordinate role at most.

The key point in the last part of the definition is "explicit interpretation." Qualitative research is synonymous with interpretative research (Ely, Anzul, Friedman, Garner, & Steinmetz, 1991; Oldfather & West, 1994). Interpretative inquiry came from a post-enlightenment tradition in Europe starting with Wilhelm Dilthey (1833-1910) and Max Weber (1864-1920) and emphasizing coming to an understanding (verstehen) of social situations. This tradition assumes that the meaning of human action is intrinsic in that action (Schwandt, 2001) while, at the same time, recognizing that there is not a universal standard agreement of "understanding." Wenger (1998, p. 41) suggests that "...understanding is always a straddling the known and the unknown in a subtle dance of the self. It is delicate balance."

Today the interpretivist tradition is exemplified by Geertz (1973) and a trend in cultural anthropology called interpretative anthropology, in which existing cultures are considered as a living text. A counterpart in social psychology and organization studies is Karl Weick (1995) and his theory of sensemaking, where a manager manipulates symbols and urges certain interpretations of events so that employees make sense of their work life. A tradition that shares some of the assumptions of interpretivism is constructivism (Berger & Luckman, 1966; Collins, 1997; Gergen, 1994; Hacking, 1999; Phillips, 2000; Potter, 1996; Sarbin & Kitsue, 1994; von Glasersfeld, 1995) but each theorist stresses a more phenomenological, philosophical orientation. In addition, each theorist has his/her own variation on similar themes, which assert that shared reality is not a matter of fact but one that is construed differently both socially and cognitively depending on our perspective and assumptions.

Within these interpretivists' traditions, my guiding research question for the purpose of the study was: "What is the organizational culture of this firm?" I have made the assumption that organizations have cultures and that these cultures make sense of symbols and events for the members of that organization (Frost, Moore, Louis, Lundberg, & Martin, 1991). The use of ethnographic methods provides the researcher a means to interpret and describe the cultural texture of that firm. It is worth noting that whether a materialistic inventory (quantitative analysis) or symbolic inventory (interpretative analysis) is conducted, the researcher still must interpret the data.

The next question was: "How does this high-tech manufacturing firm learn?" When the research began, learning was defined simply as the transfer of knowledge and/or skills from a more experienced person to a less experienced person. As the research and literature review informed my observations, I clarified the definition of learning with reference to Lave & Wenger (1991). Emphasis centers on the whole person, viewing activity, agent and context as mutually constitutive. Individuals move from the periphery of a practice to become full participants in a practice. Learning is viewed primarily as a social participation. Moreover, at an organizational level, information, knowledge, and experience result in alteration of structural configurations as the organization adapts from lessons learned.

It also should be noted that these two guiding research questions are related in that social learning theory suggests that social and cultural context constitute the learning process. Further, in light of these questions and definitions, what appears to help or hinder learning at this firm? Simply put, the research task of this study is descriptive, exploratory and interpretative.

Data Generation Procedures

Participant observations began October 2000, and continued on a near-weekly basis until April 2001. Some weeks I spent 25 hours observing and participating; other weeks I spent only two or three hours on site. My research log indicates that I spent about 90 hours at the plant with employees during the observation portion of the research. At times I sat at a workbench in the pattern shop across from one or two employees while they shaped bike helmet molds. Other times I lingered in the design room watching collaborations and random meetings merge and disperse. Still other times I would stand next to someone in the assembly area while s/he pounded vents or machined a mold. Conversations ranged from the tasks at hand, to what people thought of working at this company, to family life. My initial research goals were to learn some of their tasks, to know them personally, and to learn their view of learning in the workplace. By building rapport, I hoped to hear their unvarnished opinions of their workplace and its learning.

A research log was the main method for recording thoughts, experiences, and reflections during the participant observation segment of the research. Interpretative inquiry often is considered data generation rather than data collection since the researcher is the main instrument for inquiry (Burns-McCoy, 1999; Wax, 1971). However, if one looks critically at nearly every research process, data collection is selective, and therefore the researcher has generated what data s/he has decided to analyze (Carr & Kemmis, 1983).

With events such as new employee orientation, I elected to videotape the proceedings so I could observe better more of the details. New employee orientation was an experience that nearly all employees shared in common and provided the standard the founder and owners wished to set. Company values were discussed and expectations were explained. According to Sperschneider & Bagger (2003), prolonged engagement, provided in this case by the opportunity to review videos and transcripts, is an important element in qualitative inquiry within an industrial context.

On some occasions I participated in the work in the pattern shop, and I felt that I was accepted by the group when pattern makers asked me to put down the clipboard and pitch in. In fact, at the beginning of the fieldwork, I considered leaving my part-time job at the university so I could become more of an insider in the substantive work and learning of this company. After six months, however, the workload slowed at the research site; partial and temporary layoffs made my inquiry increasingly difficult toward the end of my fieldwork. Nevertheless, it was during this wave of layoffs and work slow-downs that I conducted my first interviews. Through informal chatting, several names repeatedly came up as influential and knowledgeable individuals. In this way I attempted to have the members of organization select those most influential to the organization.

Nine interviews were conducted. The only interview that took place on the company premises was with the owner. The other semi-structured, open-ended interviews were tape-recorded and conducted in coffee shops, employees' homes, my own home and, on a warm summer evening, on the deck of an outdoor restaurant over some beers. In one case, I drove seven hours to interview a former employee. Because of the open-ended nature of the interviews, they varied in length from one hour to three and one-half hours. Questions were asked in a way that allowed the interviewee to set the agenda, for example: "Tell me about working at Delta Technologies" or "Tell me some stories that exemplified how people learn at Delta Technologies." Also, during most interviews, I used the Organizational Learning Profile from DiBella and Nevis 1998 p. 100) as a platform to focus the interview toward learning in the organization.

Ethical Considerations

An important consideration in qualitative research is acknowledging the delicacy of not betraying a person's trust and still telling the story with nuances of virtue and vice. Employees gave their own personal time and risked their job security to be bluntly honest. Thus, it is imperative for me to be as accurate as possible with what they entrusted to me and to protect their confidentiality. Qualitative researchers depict their endeavor as "a sacred science" (Denzin & Lincoln, 1994), a trust between the researcher and those who agree to be part of a study.

Another important consideration in telling the story is individual agreements with respondents. For example, some interviewees in this particular study spoke only with the understanding that their identity would not be exposed. Others said they had "no problem" with being quoted directly. Still others indicated that if being identified would help the study and the organization, their comments could be attributed to them in the finished publication.

Protection of individual identities also had to be given because of the relatively small size of the organization. A seemingly innocuous comment could be attributed quickly to a specific employee. In one interview I mentioned the career goals of someone I had spoken with earlier, and the person with me immediately identified the previous interviewee without my having specified his name. In retrospect, this gaffe seems minor because both parties no longer work at Delta Technologies. Also, the one unintentionally identified had given me the name of the person I was presently interviewing. Nevertheless, I counted it as a lesson learned about how easy it is to unintentionally reveal sources in a small organization in a relatively small town.

Perhaps the individual who has the most to gain, and lose, from this study is the owner and founder of the organization. On the positive side, the owner has paid nothing for this in-depth research. This research can give perspective to potential blind spots and realistically may enhance the competitive advantage of his firm, free-of-charge. At the same time, I have brought to light some issues that hinder learning and could potentially embarrass the owner and the organization. Albeit I have not revealed all I discovered; to do so seemed gratuitous. I recognized that to "rummage" around in anyone's life for any length of time of may result in a less than flattering depiction of events. By keeping both the organization and participants anonymous, I hope to minimize the negatives and accentuate the positives for those involved. My goal was to discover what may be hindering learning not to dig up dirt.

The willingness of the owner to be open to this study shows an enthusiasm to learn. It is my ardent intention to provide an account that will benefit his organization and reward his appetite to learn. As I mentioned to the owner, learning often occurs after a negative event (Vaill, 1996). To deny the negative events in the learning process is to miss some important lessons in the iterative cycle.

Ethnographic Validity

Validity means different things to different researchers. For example, Creswell and Miller (2000) summarize that "...qualitative inquirers need to demonstrate that their studies are credible" (p. 124). They go on to argue that validity is guided by "...two perspectives: the lens researchers choose to validate their studies and researchers' paradigm assumptions" (p. 124). Similarly, Sanjek (1990) posits that there are three canons of ethnographic validity: theoretical candor; depiction of the ethnographic path; and field note evidence (pp. 385-418). Each of these canons of validity are found as documentation in the pages ahead to suggest the credibility of this study. Theoretical candor is described in each chapter, but primarily found in Chapters One and Two. My path as an ethnographer is explained mainly in Chapters One, Three, and Four, and my field note evidence with verbatim quotations and my interpretation are found in Chapters Three and Four.

Moreover, I suggest that the quality of qualitative research rises or falls with the integrity and honesty of the researcher. Keeping one's word is the baseline for generating a story that rings true and that provides a perspective that will enable this organization to enhance its learning.

Researcher as Instrument

The concept of the researcher as instrument is unique to qualitative research (Ely, et al., 1991). It is through the researcher's lenses that data are gathered, sorted, generated and interpreted. The perspectives and biases of the researcher need to be lucid and articulated so that what the researcher reports is fully acknowledged as his or her point of view. The qualitative researcher does not merely point to the questionnaire as the measuring instrument; the researcher is the instrument for the research. There is an intrinsic sense of ownership for what is learned and explained in the research process. Therefore, it is incumbent upon a qualitative researcher to reveal the biases he or she brings to the research project.

Although a quantitative approach would have been more expedient, I have chosen a qualitative approach because my bachelor and Master of Arts degrees are in cultural anthropology. The first book I read at San Diego State University was Thomas Kuhn's (1970) The Structures of Scientific Revolutions, one of most influential and widely cited books in academe. Kuhn (1970) argues that scientific discoveries and revolution take place embedded in human communities. These scientific communities inculcate future scientists into methods of conducting research and, on a tacit level, the ways the communities perceive their research (Rorty, 1999). This is where the term "paradigm" emerged. Scientific revolutions, therefore, occur not during "normal science," but when a substantial amount of data does not fit the accepted paradigm and a new community forms that is willing to hold in abeyance the conventional wisdom and test different sets of hypotheses. More than 20 years ago I reasoned that if the so-called hard sciences squabble over paradigms, the study of humans, with a multitude of competing paradigms, requires a more sagacious and human approach to understanding mutual human endeavors and predicaments.

In the same vein, I concur with Hanson's axiom that "all data are theory-laden" (Barbour, 1972). Whether in a controlled laboratory environment or drafting a questionnaire, data are yielded with a specific null hypothesis to test. A controlled environment tests a certain theory and a certain hypothesis. Data do not speak for themselves; they give voice to a script written by the researcher. It is through parameters set by the controls and hypothesis that data yield their information. For instance, consider the etymology of the word "fact." Originally, the connotations of this word suggest that facts were produced by actions (see Oxford English Dictionary, 1989, vol. V, p. 651).

Nevertheless, in researching the efficacy of a medical procedure or medication, for example, quantitative research methods do have a privileged place, in my opinion. The object of a study allows and stipulates what instrument to use in the research process in light of what questions are being asked. Anthropologist Clifford Geertz reasons that although objectivity, like absolute sterility, is not possible with the study of humans, that does not mean we should conduct surgery in a sewer (1973, p. 30).

When conducting a naturalistic study of an organization, the researcher's points of view will be woven into the finished fabric of the final report (Burns-McCoy, 1999). It is, therefore, academically sound to explain philosophically and practically what presuppositions the researcher brings to the research project. Explaining my biases is one means of being forthright about any personal agendas.

Philosophically, I would place myself solidly in the social constructivist, pragmatist and interpretivist camp, which will be explained in more detail in Chapter Two. When I was in my early 20s studying cultural anthropology, I had the realization that I did not decide on the culture in which I was raised or the socialization I experienced as a child; my socialization would have been categorically different had I been brought up in India or China. This seems obvious now, but the recognition that forces and structures shaped my identity and virtually everything I held to be true, assuaged the dogmatism and naive realism that I smugly held. This personal realization was both disconcerting and emancipatory as I recognized some of my epistemological and situational limits.

More recently I have appreciated how deeply ingrained working-class values played a part in my development as an individual. Lubrano (2004) chronicles the tension for the offspring of working class, blue-collar families who must negotiate a different set of values as they enter college and the white-collar world work. Lubrano (2004) describes the experience of "straddles" as they grapple with a duality that exits within them and their social world. At times there is a deliberate abandonment of certain working-class values and acceptance of white-collar values. Often, however, often there is uneasiness with the limitations each class orientation.

I was reared in a working-class home. My father was a skilled cabinet builder/carpenter who later became a contractor and successful small business owner in San Diego, California. Perhaps it was my father's poor judgment of character, or perhaps his hesitance to pay high enough wages to attract and retain quality employees, but I saw my father go through dozens of employees. They stole both from him and his customers; they came to work drunk, if they showed up at all. Therefore, one value I gleaned from growing up in this household and business was that reliable employees were the most valuable assets for our family business.

Another lesson I learned was about education. My father appeared to me to be held back by not being educated past the eighth grade. He seemed to lack the confidence to expand his business and take larger contracts. For instance, when my father needed to write business or personal checks, he needed a crib sheet with the cardinal numbers spelled out. Although I did not start college until I was 25, I quickly came to value the freedom and confidence learning provides. Thus, learning and responsibility are woven deeply into my values. And while I grew up with the perspective of the boss's kid (i.e., management), I also saw abysmal, irresponsible management above me while I spent five years as a maintenance supervisor before I started my doctoral studies. I can identify with managers and owners, since my father was both and was taken advantage of, and I have also seen management treat employees with contempt for no apparent reason other than that they could. It is my resolute desire to see work places as healthy, positive environments where individuals can actualize their human potential and where the relationship between labor and management can be genuinely respectful and mutually beneficial.

Delimitations and Limitations

This ethnographic study explores learning and the conditions that promote or hinder learning at a single organization in the Pacific Northwest. Ethnographic studies are bound in time and space by the historical and economic cycles of organization and by the limits of concluding a research report. In a naturalistic study (Lincoln & Guba, 1985), there is an arbitrary condition as to when the researcher must decide that data are repeating themselves (Wolcott, 1990) and determine that whatever lessons have been learned are concluded. There comes a point on the iterative learning cycle at which one must step off and write up the experience. This is both a necessity and a limitation.

Another boundary to be delineated is the research design affiliated with naturalistic inquiry. Rather than stressing reliability and external validity, as in quantitative studies, this study focuses on trustworthiness of the data and transferability of the results. However, qualitative details are by nature interpretative and contextual. The transferability or applicability of the lessons learned in this study will depend on how similar other situations may be. Trustworthiness of data may be related if "the research narrative contains the textual and structural description necessary to allow others to reach their own conclusions concerning whether or not transfer is a possibility to other work environments" (Deems, 1997, p.18).

A more specific limitation resulted from the combination of finding a research site, my eagerness to start the research project, and my inexperience in understanding some common pitfalls of stakeholders. The task of gaining permission to study an organization in-depth proved more difficult than I anticipated. Several early leads fell through for various reasons, such as funding issues or logistical problems with travel or language. When an organization near home showed interest, I felt I was not in a position to be selective and not confident enough to suggest or negotiate more ideal conditions.

In my field notes from my first face-to-face meeting with the owner, in which I explained my research methodology, I wrote that the owner said, "I'm interested." Rather than proceeding to negotiate what exactly this research might include, I gratefully accepted his interest as approval to begin research. I was welcomed in and given a tour of operations that afternoon. Some particulars were discussed; however, unexpected conditions and impediments became evident later. I was introduced first by e-mail to the employees; a prior commitment prevented me from attending an all-shop meeting at which I would have been introduced in person.

The day I began observations the owner told me "not to take people away from their work." I could appreciate the owner's concern, but this abrupt limitation forced me to interview employees on their own time. In retrospect, this limitation did not prove difficult to overcome. For one thing, the ambient noise made it nearly impossible to tape interviews in the shop. I also believe that those interviewed spoke more candidly than they would have on site. The limitation of "not taking people away from their work" also compelled me to seek out former employees to interview; it is hard to imagine current employees sharing the critical comments that former employees shared with me. Lastly, this limitation compelled me to build rapport even more intensely since I knew that, in the future

I would need to ask certain people for their own time to conduct interviews. It is difficult to explain how the lack of support I felt from some key members of the management team affected the research. I made the erroneous assumption that if the owner agreed to the research, others on the management teams also would agree. The rank and file employees were gregarious and accepting of my inquiry; however, with three key management employees, I felt like an unwelcome guest. By not paying closer attention to these key stakeholders, I limited their perspective into this study. Of course, these individuals had little to gain and more to lose from being under a microscope and perhaps, regardless of what I did, these individuals may have kept their guard up. It is likely that each had his/her own issues about why I was perceived as a threat or a nuisance. It is difficult, in retrospect, to see how I could have overcome these managers' reserve or been able to see their resistance in advance. Perhaps a brief meeting with the managers and owner to answer questions and gain a greater "buy in" to the research process would have been productive. Hindsight is always more clear.

Another limitation that emerged was my access to e-mail discussions between staff. While I can appreciate wanting to keep sensitive issues private, this limitation restrained another data source. What I learned in the process is indicative what I was faced with in my overall attempt to understand Delta Technologies. When I first asked to be put on an e-mail list, the financial controller was incredulous. "What do you want to know?" She asked defensively "Well," I explained, "for the purpose of my research I want to learn how things work, along with what the problems are." The controller shot back, "We know what our problems are," she said as her voice trailed off—concerned that I might continue to probe. I surmised I had simply asked the wrong person.

Later the same day, I talked with the owner about being placed on some distribution lists. Initially, my request was again met with resistance, and I reminded him that he had asked me to look at the "underbelly" of Delta Technologies. The owner's response was, "You don't need to go through each piece of shit in a sewer pipe to know what goes down the toilet." "True," I replied, "but I do need access to the toilet." The owner shifted his weight from foot to foot, clearly uncomfortable with this discussion. At that moment, I felt like the wagons were forming a circle. In hindsight, I admit I was not surprised, but nevertheless a bit disappointed with the defensive routine. Later that day the human resource manager asked what distribution list I would like to be added to, so I picked from a menu such as training and quality. Yet the story does not end here.

I received over 1000 e-mails in the six months that I read and coded. However these e-mails appeared sanitized, mundane, and largely devoid of human passion and structural problems. I remarked during an interview with a highly regarded former employee that these e-mails also seemed "edited or screened before they were sent out to me." He said he would be surprised if they weren't. In light of this information I decided to eliminate the e-mail as data source, except for what is noted here.

The last limitation was the use of the Organizational Learning Profile (see DiBella and Nevis 1998 p. 100). When I asked if I could administer the instrument during an all-staff meeting, my request was denied by the Production Manager. The reason given was that the instrument was too complicated and would take up too much time. So, since I was not allowed to take people away from their work, I limited the use of the profile except during some interviews to add structure and a springboard for theoretical issues.

Nevertheless, none of these limitations proved insurmountable to the research project. They are mentioned to explain why some paths were taken, while other paths were not explored. The next chapter will explore some patterns in the field of organizational learning and communities of practice to provide some theoretical back ground for this study.

CHAPTER TWO

Patterns in the Literature

An organization is a body of thought thought by thinking thinkers.

Karl Weick, 1979a, p. 42

The Pattern Making Shop

The different patterns in the shape of a bike helmet are relatively similar to each other to the untrained eye, but slight design differentiation is no small matter for bike helmet manufacturers. The slightest nuances of shapes and designs are considered proprietary, so much so that when one customer pays a visit to Delta Technologies, thick sheets of black plastic cover the shelves of patterns in the production process. Clipboards hung on walls with information on projects are flipped around. Ideas and designs clearly have a value and that value is protected. The message implied to customers is that their ideas and designs will be protected.

The proximity of the Design Shop to the Pattern Shop suggests a continuation of the design process. Ideas become objects for rigorous examination. An acceptable pattern not only must have a smooth surface and a symmetrical shape that matches the customer's exact specifications, the shape also must allow molten aluminum to flow into and fill each cavity of the pattern. The term used to describe this process is "to draft." If the cavity does not draft, the pattern is useless and must be poured again and perhaps reshaped or redesigned. The distinctions are subtle, and apart from experience the only sure test is doing a pour in the foundry.

Moving from the Design Shop to the Pattern Shop a visitor's senses are struck by the smell of resin and sawdust. The ambient noise is modulated as saws or drill presses are used, or as an air compressor motor periodically cycles off and on. People sit at workbenches, concentrating on their work, while chatting and listening to the radio. At one workstation there is "classic" rock playing, while classical music fills the air of another. There is a thin layer of dust on nearly everything, although the area is swept at least once a day. The general ambiances is of humorous rapid-fire conversation where nothing is off limits, such as politics and religion, but is more likely centered on hunting, fishing, music, and especially work; discussion of work is a theme of apparent genuine interest.

Project managers will step in to check a pattern mold while they are in the area, or more likely a project manager will be asked to look over a mold. It is common for four or five people to stare at a mold design without saying a word for several minutes. When the more experienced person with, for example, six years of experience finally speaks, he uses a specialized vocabulary. Those in the circle dip their heads and bend their ears to catch the words being spoken; with the ambient noise, listening does require extra effort. After the project manager/ sale representative departs and the group breaks up, I ask the man with two years experience what the project manager with more experience had said in this huddle. He says, with a serious but blank look on his face, "I'm not really sure." The person who admitted his confusion is a bright, thoughtful fellow who cares about the quality of his work. The uncertainty centers on a knowledge domain that is technical, specialized, and partially tactic. It seems remarkable that after two years in practice, this pattern maker appeared reticent to ask for clarification, and that the project manager did not ask for the pattern maker to repeat what he had heard. It was as if these two employees did not share a common language.

Introduction

To explain and interpret the organization depicted above, it is first necessary to review the patterns of thought in a body of literature pertinent to the research topic. The conceptual patterns will be discussed and explained to support why this particular research design was selected for the project at Delta Technologies. The patterns to be explored in the literature of organizational learning share similarities with efforts in the Pattern Shop at Delta Technologies to flesh out the design. For instance, after the Design Shop has completed its work, the Pattern Shop turns the concept into an object. The abstract formulas and shapes from the computer screen are manifest as a tangible item with texture and substance. Similar to the Pattern Shop at Delta Technologies where ideas are given substance, this chapter will explore some literary patterns of organizational learning and how these ideas apply to the research design for exploring Delta Technologies.

The literature of organizational learning exhibits certain patterns and guises that can be traced and explicated. The main difficulty in reviewing the literature of organizational learning centers on the prodigious volume and proliferation of documents of the field. The fact that organizational learning is an inter-disciplinary bailiwick adds to the burden of understanding this dynamic field. The disciplinary diversity is evidenced in the number of graduate theses and dissertations that have "organizational learning" in their title or abstract; from 1972 until June 2002, approximately 400 graduate theses and dissertations have been written with "organizational learning" in the title and/or abstract. Roughly half of the research topics are in the field of education and half are related to business and management topics.

Writing about the growth of articles published on organizational learning, Crossan and Guatto (1996) enumerated the exponential growth of publications in the field. Crossan and Guatto also note the articles most often cited as influential to organizational learning's development. Their research included publications though 1994, with about 60 publications each year. Ten years later the exponential growth pattern continues. I conducted a basic search on the EBSCO academic database in January 2004 and had approximately 2,000 hits. If the search parameters are broadened, the results net as many as 20,000 references. In addition, the 1,900 journal titles in the EBSCO database are by no means a comprehensive list of the number of publications available. Ulrich's Serials Directory contains approximately 250,000 titles that are published by 80,000 entities worldwide. Roughly half of these titles are considered academic, 32,000 of which are peer-reviewed. Titles listed online, most of which are available in paper as well, also number 32,000. Using these figures, EBSCO's 1,900 titles represent roughly 6% of the available online journals.

The copious number of articles underscores the need for organizational learning and knowledge management to be practiced and not merely studied. Information and knowledge nowadays can inundate most any endeavor. Knowledge management is a field that has some shared interests with organizational learning and will be alluded to in more detail later in this chapter. The number of books on organizational learning is likewise relatively substantial and expanding. A simple search on Amazon.com (which many librarians use as source of books in print) retrieves 289 titles when a search is conducted with key words "organizational learning." So, how do we make sense of this rapidly expanding field? Understanding the idea of "learning" is a beneficial place to start.

Learning

Some distinctions are needed with such an enormous topic as "learning." Learning may be considered to fall into four major schools of thought, as represented in Appendix A. By and large, most of the theorists and schools of thought mentioned below agree that learning is "the acquiring of knowledge or skills" (Webster's New World Dictionary, p. 796). Disagreements emerge concerning which methods or means of learning are the most advantageous, and where the emphasis should be placed if learning is a goal.

Learning is broadly defined in this research project is the process in which understanding, performance or skills are enhanced through reflection, interactions with others, or purposeful instruction. The learning process may consist of both formal and informal methods and may be intentional or inadvertent. Rooted in action and social relations, the learning process thrives as practice meshes with conversation. Social connections provide a bridge for knowledge to transfer between participants.

In some respects, social learning is as old as the Socratic method of instruction by questioning. Nothing replaces the vital social interaction between humans to understand an issue or a skill. As a Hebrew proverb puts it, "As iron sharpens iron, so one man sharpens another" (Proverbs 27:17). This earthy simile suggests that friction and sparks emerge from interactions but, nevertheless, result in sharpness and focus in a person's character and actions.

The research in this project stresses the importance of social/ situational learning. Russian psychologist Lev Vygotsky (1896-1934) first explored social learning with children. He was born the same year as Piaget, yet for political reasons and because of his early demise, his writings only recently have reached Western scholars. Similar to Piaget, Vygotsky explored how differences shape the structural and cognitive processes in children. However, Vygotsky saw social activity, instead of individual discovery, as key to learning. Vygotsky stressed shared intellectual tools, such as language, when dealing with tasks. Piaget, on the other hand, pointed toward transformations of perspectives that suggested progression in cognitive abilities such as counting or physical reasoning.

Educational researcher Rogoff (1990) contrasts the differences between Vygotsky and Piaget as follows:

> Vygotsky focuses on shared problem solving, in which the partners collaborate to reach a joint solution to problems, whereas Piaget focuses on reciprocal examination of logical statements by partners. With Vygotsky, the cognitive process is shared between people; with Piaget, the social process provides individuals with the opportunity to see alternatives and to explore the logical consequences of their own position, in a meeting of minds as opposed to a shared thinking process. (p.192)

According to Vygotsky, shared cultural goals provide the impetus for learning to occur, contrasted with Piagetan emphasis on individual cognitive and rational development. It is understandable that organizational learning, which may be considered as collective learning, resonates with social learning theory. Following Vygotsky, Bandura's (1977) social learning theory posited that: "People learn from observing other people; by definition, such observations take place in a social setting" (Merriam & Caffarella, 1991/1998, p. 134 cited in Smith, 2003c). Observations allow us to see the consequences of action without participation, which can limit some of the difficulty and hazards of learning something the first time. Seeing a model provides a template for future actions and eliminates or limits likely mistakes.

Lave and Wenger (1991) push the social learning model further to what they call "situational learning." Instead of seeing learning as the obtaining of certain skills or knowledge, they have placed relationships and participation at the center of the learning context. It is the situation in which participants move from "legitimate peripheral participation" to full participation in a community of practitioners. Situated learning will be discussed in the latter part of this chapter under the communities of practice rubric.

Multiple Perspectives of Organization Studies— A Preview

Due to the enormous body of research in the domain of organizational learning, the notion of a comprehensive literature review must give way to a more modest review of some leading contributors to the field of organizational learning. Organizational learning encompasses educational psychology, social psychology, sociology, anthropology, organization studies, and management studies. Agreeing with Hatch (1997) and her emphasis on multiple perspectives in organization theory, I will use the broad paradigms of modern, interpretative, and critical theories to organize this literature review. Smircich and Calás (1987) take a similar approach in their assessment of organizational culture. The boundaries between these paradigms, however, are viewed as being porous, allowing different perspectives to enliven cross-paradigmatic conversations. Since organizational learning is interdisciplinary, one goal of this chapter is to explain the various roots of this discipline.

The perspectives of modern, interpretative, and critical organizational theory need to be thought of as broad and suggestive categories. The exploration of a forest of ideas serves as an apt metaphor to explain some theoretical landscapes. On closer examination, many of the theorists in the pages ahead incorporate two or sometimes even all three perspectives into their writings. There is certainly room for disagreement among theoretical interpretations. Still other theorists, such as Hatch (1997) and Morgan (1986), transcend these categories by the survey nature of their seminal work. It is important to note that these perspectives are mere tools to organize and understand what has been written in the past. A brief overview of each perspective will be introduced, followed by a chronological presentation of some of the main contributors to the idea of organizational learning and communities of practice.

Modernist Perspective

Modern organizational theory is broadly defined here as a traditional scientific perspective in which rationality and reduction are held to yield answers to problems and hypotheses. Modern organizational theory perspective assumes that life is orderly and moving toward greater progress when using positivistic methods for explanation of phenomena. Another theme of modern organization theory is that of control. Kuhn (1970) considered modern notions akin to "normal science," where small experiments are placed together to build or support large theories. Terms like "principles" and "foundations" of knowledge occur often, whereas in earlier years modernists spoke of laws of nature, like gravity.

Smircich and Calás (1987) refer to this paradigm as functionalist: each part of society has a function and those functions affect each other.

Fredrick Winslow Taylor (The Principles of Scientific Management, 1913) provides an example of classic early modernist theory. The contemporary modernist speaks more in terms of a systems approach to academic disciplines. Modern sensibilities emerged in the context of the industrial revolution where science and technology controlled and predicted progress. It was not until issues such as pollution or events like Three Mile Island, Chernobyl or the Challenger disaster that suggested technology might have unforeseen ramifications. Epistemological limits were considered only temporary in the modern quest for mastery. The general attitude toward our modern scientific knowledge in many academic or business communities is positivist in practice, with rare acknowledgment of epistemological limits. Those who value what science can do, yet who also acknowledge the limits to the reliability of knowledge are growing in number (Arygis, 1980; Barbour, 1974; Kuhn, 1970, Polanyi, 1958; Polkinghorne, 1996; Rorty, 1979). As the list of skeptics of modernism grew longer, the differences between those theories with modernist assumptions evolved to recognize the limits of modern scientific knowledge. For instance, a modern systems approach may blend into a more interpretative and constructionist perspective, such as Weick's notion of enactment and sensemaking (1995), yet still value some modern sensibilities of systems mapping. It is in the interplay between paradigms, according to Hatch (1997), where interesting insights emerge.

Interpretative/ Symbolic Perspectives

An interpretative organizational perspective, again broadly defined, suggests that there is more to life than meets the eye. As with a traffic accident that provokes multiple versions of what just occurred, interpretivists suggest that one point of view limits our understanding of a phenomenon, and that there are often multiple interpretations. Rather than seeing organizational life as a series of problems to be solved, interpretivists see organizational life as consisting of mysteries and narratives to be understood (Eisenberg & Goodall, 1993, p. 124). Interpretivists consider that assumptions affect one's perspective, similar to the notion in Heisenberg's uncertainty principle in physics where the researcher determines what will be measured and what must be left unknown. Most often assumptions are neither perceptible to the person with the emotion, nor rational in any comprehensive sense. The ability to empathize with others and their emotional state assists an interpretivist in understanding and explaining different points of view. Interpretivists readily admit that their interpretations are not definitive. An important assumption of an interpretative perspective is that of conditional relativism; an event needs to be understood within the particular values of a culture or an organization (Geertz, 1973).

Also within the interpretative framework is the concept of social contructionism that began with the landmark work The Social Construction of Reality (Berger & Luckman, 1966). Since then, social contructionism has been explicated in fields such as philosophy (Goodman, 1978), literacy (Cook-Gumperz, 1986), gender (Lorber & Farrell, 1991), and scientific facts in the lab (Latour & Woolgar, 1979), to the point that the construction metaphor may be past its usefulness. Hewitt (2001, p. 419) questions in reviewing Hacking's (1999) book whether social contructionism might be "...another instance of sociologists' penchant for picking up stray metaphors and keeping them as house pets even when they pee on the rug and scratch the upholstery?" Hewitt (2001) continues with a pet metaphor and elaborates on why an interpretative framework is useful to understand human endeavors and on how slippery an analysis of reality can be:

> Human acts, always social, sculpt reality from materials encountered en route to their completion. Some of these materials we have already created, though we may not see our authorship when we encounter them. Other materials are not humanly created and lie beyond our control— or as least are out of our control at certain times. We respond to them on the basis of our ideas about

them, but they do not respond to us on the basis of our ideas about them. What we sculpt this "reality" to be is probing, tentative, partial and incomplete, useful for some purposes but not others. Human beings doggedly pursue "reality," which refuses to sit or stay on command (p. 421).

Critical Theory and Post-Modernism

Critical or post-modern perspective is even more unruly to define. Postmodernism radically relativizes any notion of human knowledge that attempts to build an integrated vision. A major theme to critical or post-modern thought is one of fragmentation. Richard Tarnas (1991) lists the sources in the analysis of language that have contributed to a profoundly skeptical epistemology:

> Of the many factors that have converged to this intellectual position it has been the analysis of language that has brought forth the most radically skeptical epistemological currents in the postmodern mind, and it is these currents that have identified themselves most articulately and self consciously as "postmodern." Again many sources contribute to this development — Nietzsche's analysis of the problematic relation of language to reality; C. S. Peirce's semiotics, positing all human thought takes place in signs; Ferdinand de Saussure's linguistics positing the arbitrary relationship between word and object, sign and signified; Wittgenstein's analysis of the linguistic structuring of human experience; Heidegger's existentialist-linguistic critique of metaphysics; Edward Sapir and B.L. Whorf's linguistics hypothesis that language shapes the perceptions of reality as much as reality shapes language; Michael Foucault's genealogical investigations into the social construction of knowledge; and Derrida's deconstructionism, challenging the attempt to establish a secure meaning in any text. The upshot of these several influences, particularly in the contemporary academic world, has been the dynamic dissemination of a view of human discourse and knowledge that radically relativizes human claims to a sovereign or enduring truth, and that thereby supports an emphatic revision of the character and goals of intellectual analysis. (p. 398)

If anything, postmodernism is better defined by what it does not affirm. The idea is that any single, all-encompassing and unifying explanation is not plausible in the postmodern mindset. There is what could be modestly called "small truths." Lyotard (1984) contemptuously refers to the position that truths can be construed into an integrated whole as a grand narrative. Postmodernists also attack as the modern idea of progress. If knowledge is fragmented by multiplicity of perspectives and full of contradictions, the idea that society is improving and evolving is merely wishful thinking. The fragmentation of knowledge is simply the postmodern condition. Who has not tried to make sense of the multiplicity of perspectives on a controversy such as rebuilding the World Trade Center? Each perspective has equally valid points of view.

Ironically, postmodern criticism carries ideas that cut both ways. The grand narrative that Lyotard (1984) ridicules may be seen as the grand criticism of every idea, including postmodernism. In other words, the only integrated vision is one that deconstructs modern sensibilities. In some respects, a postmodern dogmatism has merely replaced a modernist dogmatism. As Tarnas (1991) puts it: "Implicitly, one postmodern absolute is critical consciousness, which, by deconstructing all, seems compelled by its own logic to do so to itself as well. This is the unstable paradox that permeates the postmodern mind" (ibid., p. 402).

Organizational learning literature is composed in each of these three perspectives: modern, interpretative, and postmodern. Many authors share more than one perspective and see the value that each perspective brings to the table of organizational learning. The following pages will review the organizational learning literature organized by a historical progression of thinkers and their ideas in light of these three perspectives.

Scientific Management

The roots of organizational learning are evident in what has been coined "scientific management." When Fredrick Winslow Taylor (1856-1915) wrote Principles of Scientific Management (1913), he considered the movement toward increasing productivity and efficiency as an industrial juggernaut. Henry Ford started mass production of automobiles the same year Taylor published his seminal work (Tarnus, 1991). The unprecedented industrial expansion from 1880-1920, coupled with ruthless treatment of employees gave rise to Marxism and the labor movement. Poor relations between management and labor led Taylor to analyze the work process in factories. The idea of time/motion studies connoted that analysis and learning, not only revolution or strikes, can improve processes.

Ironically, Taylor worked to improve the relations between management and labor, yet he was labeled "the enemy of the working man" (Morgan, 1986, p. 30). Trained as an engineer from the middle class, Taylor's own words suggest that he attempted to improve the plight of the working class. Rather than stay in the zero-sum gain of the prevailing mentality, which he called old style management, Taylor urged management to learn how to treat employees with respect:

> The wise manager, under the old type of management, deliberately sets out to do something better for his workmen than his competitors are doing, better than he himself has ever done before... When he sets out to do better for his men than other people do for theirs, the workmen respond liberally when that time comes. I refer to this case as being the highest type of management, the case in which the managers deliberately set out to do something better for their workmen than other people are doing, and to give them a special incentive of some kind, to which the workmen respond by giving a share at least of their initiative. (Taylor, 1916, in Corman, Banks, Bantz, & Mayer, 1990, p. 69)

Note Taylor's use of the term "wise manager" in his exhortation. Wisdom is the result of learning from experience and enables prediction and foresight. The passage above urges a manager who is still in the pall of "old type management" to shift to "the highest type of management." These do not sound like the words of man attempting to oppress workers. Instead, Taylor is urging management to change its way of thinking. The importance of "mental models" popularized by Senge (1990) was intimated nearly 80 years prior by Taylor:

> The new outlook that comes under scientific management is this:
> The workmen, after many object lessons, come to see and the
> management come to see that this surplus [profit] can be made so
> great, will stop their fighting and will push as hard as they can to
> get as cheap an output as possible, that there is no reason to
> quarrel. Each side can get more than ever before. The
> acknowledgement of this fact represents a complete mental
> revolution. (Taylor, 1916, cited in Corman, et al., 1990, p. 69)

Taylor suggests that this "new outlook" or "mental revolution" emerges after
learning or in his terms, "after many object lessons." The lessons learned by
Taylor came from experience, in attempting to see the conceptual models that
were not working. Themes such as "understanding our mental models" (Senge,
1990), "changing internally before change can occur organizationally" (Bridges,
1991), and "beginning with the end in mind" (Covey, 1989) are all constructed on
Taylor's foundation.

The limits of scientific management center on the mechanical metaphor
that dominated organizational thinking in Taylor's day (Morgan, 1986). In the
situation with brute labor and highly repetitive tasks, the time/ motion studies of
scientific management saw people as interchangeable cogs within the
organizational machinery. The newly invented assembly line augmented the idea
of unskilled workers as a machine, albeit a machine that must be rested and well
fed to keep productivity up (Scott, 1998, p. 98). Presently, however, such a
reducetionistic approach reveals its obsolescence with specialized skills with
numerous contingencies, or knowledge work that requires creativity and high-
level problem solving with knowledge generation. Nowadays, employees are not
only motivated by salary, but by the quality of the workplace, a sense of
community, and the opportunity for professional growth. It is easy to judge
scientific management harshly by today's standards, but we must keep in mind
that human knowledge is limited by its situation. Moreover, Taylor's ideas also
were often associated with those of Henry Ford in that productivity ideas were
divorced from equity. For example, the automobile plants of Ford sustained an
average 380 percent turnover under scientific management (Morgan, 1986, p. 31).

Nevertheless, Taylor saw relationships between management and employees as the key element to organizational improvement and productivity. This relationship connection with the edification of an organization is inherently tied to learning from experience. Learning is what changes minds, which in turn changes practices and routines of organizations into more productive actions.

Kurt Lewin and Systems Thinking

It would take several decades for the machine metaphor to give way to a cybernetic model for modern organizations. System thinking would eventually become the "fifth discipline" for the learning organization proposed by Senge (1990). An improved relationship, suggested by Taylor provides a feedback interchange so that learning and improvement may take place.

If there is one central thesis that characterizes organizational learning, it would be a feedback model that serves as a method of correction and change, in essence, for learning from mistakes or problems. System thinking and the notion of feedback can be tracked back to the cybernetics of Wiener (1961). Carr (1997) elaborates on the roots of cybernetics:

> In the 1940s he [Wiener] used imagery from the Greek term meaning a "steersman", i.e. kubernetes, in his founding of the area of cybernetics. The steersman maintains control over his craft through knowledge to make corrections to the direction of the craft required "reading" of its current course and directing the rudder in the exact opposite to that responsible for it being "off course". For Wiener and others who were contributing to these founding years of cybernetics, such as von Bertalanffy (1956), achieving control required understanding of the broader system that was involved, including an appreciation of that system's environment. (p. 225)

The sailing imagery of ongoing navigational corrections in light of wind speed and direction, currents and tides suggests a dynamic involvement to maintain control. In the biological sciences, we can exchange the word "homeostasis" (the balance of a steady state) with "control." Whether it is the physical properties of a single cell or the entire balance of life in the forest ecological system, there are feedback loops that attempt to keep the system "controlled." System thinking or, more precisely, system models diffused to social sciences such as psychology and management studies.

German gestalt psychologist Kurt Lewin (1890-1947) applied a system feedback model from electrical engineering to group dynamics and became the chief progenitor of ideas that emerged as the notion of organizational learning. Lewin was a seminal thinker and had enormous impact on the field of social psychology. Eventually ending up at M.I.T. and establishing a Research Center on Group Dynamics, Lewin also inspired the founding of the National Training Laboratories shortly before his death at the age of 57. Anyone who has been in training sessions with a list of ideas on large sheets of paper taped to the wall has come under the influence of Lewin. As Kleiner (1996) writes:

> Nearly every sincere effort to improve organizations from within can be traced back to him, often through a thicket of tangled, hidden influences. His work spread from mentor to student, from consultant to manager to colleague, always through the medium of small groups. (p. 30)

It was Lewin who suggested that: "You cannot know an institution until you try to change it, and you cannot change it without reflecting on its purpose" (Kleiner, 1996, p. 30). Lewin developed a three-stage model for social change. Holding that social forces were frozen against each other, one wanting change and another group resisting change, he described the social dynamic as being in a state of "quasi-stationary equilibrium" (Carr, 1997, p. 225). Unfreezing occurred when the equilibrium was thrown off by a change in resistance or dissatisfaction with the current situation (Lewin, 1951). During the unfrozen state, change was introduced by training for a new behavioral pattern or a reporting relationship with a more participatory management style. Once the new norms were accepted, the so-called refreezing took place as the new ideas were institutionalized.

Argyris and Schön (1996, p. 44) attribute action research to Lewin, where participants of an organization conduct inquiry with a view of actuating organizational change. Lewin (1948) summarized the first step in the action research learning cycle:

> The first step then is to examine the idea carefully in the light of the means available. Frequently more fact-finding about the situation is required. If this first period of planning is successful, two items emerge: namely, "an overall plan" of how to reach the objective and secondly, a decision in regard to the first step of action. Usually this planning has also somewhat modified the original idea. Next, one "composed of a circle of planning, executing, and reconnaissance or fact finding for the purpose of evaluating the results of the second step, and preparing the rational basis for planning the third step, and for perhaps modifying again the overall plan." (pp. 205-206)

Students of education will notice iteration similarities of Dewey's (1933) experiential learning, Kolb's learning cycle (Kolb, 1984) and Deming or Shewhart's learning cycle (Deming, 1986, p. 88).

Action research was only one of the ways that Lewin attempted to bridge theory with practice. Gordon Allport, who wrote the introduction to Resolving Social Conflicts (Lewin, 1948, p. xi) suggests that the desire for integration of theory and practice was one of the many ideas shared by John Dewey and Kurt Lewin. Dewey's ideas influenced the following scholars, who published the first book with organizational learning in its title: Donald Schön of M.I.T. and Chris Arygris of Harvard.

Argyris

Chris Argyris came into contact with Kurt Lewin while completing his undergraduate degree in psychology at Clark University in Worcester,

Massachusetts (Smith, 2003a). Arygris went on to complete a Ph.D. in Organizational Behavior at Cornell, where he studied under William Whyte, author of The Organization Man (1956). This widely acclaimed book was a trenchant critique of executives whose lives are so banal they "sell out" and become company men.

Argyris' earliest research examined the impact of rigid organization structures on individuals and their response and adaptation to these larger systems. This analysis was presented in Personality and Organization (1957) and Integrating the Individual and the Organization (1964). His research then turned toward organizational change and the role of senior executives in the organization with Interpersonal Competence and Organizational Effectiveness (1962) and Organization and Innovation (1965). Arygris went on to rethink social research and the role of the researcher in the research process with Intervention Theory and Method (1970), Inner Contradiction of Rigorous Research (1980), and Action Science (1985). It was during this time that Argyris moved from Yale (1951-1971) to Harvard (1971- present) and his collaboration with Donald Schön began.

One prominent concept that Argyris and Schön posited is that each person has a mental map of how the world works and how they should behave to navigate in it. The mental map concept appears to have emerged from distillation of earlier research on the interaction between individuals and organizations. Mental maps also are known in other terms such as "worldview" (used in anthropology and philosophy) (Kearney, 1984). The concept includes assumptions about planning, engagement of those plans, and review of what occurs after the engagement and why. Moreover, Argyris and Schön distinguished between theories-in-use and espoused theories. Theories-in-use pertains to actions that are actually linked to practice or behavior one can observe. For instance, action that values planning would be seen in the use of blueprints and schedules. If an organization merely espouses planning, but deadlines are insignificant or materials are not ordered, then planning may be correctly seen as having little importance. Another way to express this distinction is between active values and passive values.

The lack of congruence between theories-in-use and espoused theories is not necessarily harmful unless the gap becomes so pronounced that excessive effort is needed to defend the incongruence. In most cases, the incongruence is material for reflection, dialogue, and learning to increase effectiveness. In the primary terms of Argyris and Schön, "organizational learning involves the detection and correction of errors" (1978, p. 2), labeled as single-loop learning. This detection and correction involves mundane issues of organizational life. A problem is identified, and steps are taken to correct the problem. This simple feedback loop, or single loop learning, is a clear example of how system thinking affected Argyris and Schön's thought. The example they give is of a thermostat that keeps a room at a certain temperature, keeping the system in balance.

In the case where incongruence between words and deeds is ample, a predictable result will likely involve defensiveness. When policies and procedures in an organization result in a gap between what is said and what is actually done (theories-in-use and espoused theories), Argyris (1990) describes this dynamic as organizational defensiveness. The system balance is seriously out of kilter, suggesting the need for double loop learning. Along with simple reflection on the problem, the entire feedback loop or learning loop needs to be reconstituted. A system blockage has occurred that does not allow for single loop detection and connection to take place. The first feedback loop has become blind to examination. The first learning system must be reconfigured by the second loop learning and inquiry, which detects and corrects the first loop's dysfunction. Gregory Bateson (1972) calls this "learning how to learn" or "deuterolearning," which comes from Greek, meaning secondary or distance (Webster's New World Dictionary, p. 376). The image is one of stepping back and getting a larger perspective.

The key step to gaining a broader perspective is reflection, or in contemporary parlance, reflexivity. The simple act of stepping back and gaining perspective is the one essential mode for professionals to learn, according to Schön in his classic *The Reflective Practitioner: How Professionals Think in Action* (1983).

Schön

Donald A. Schön graduated from Yale with a degree in philosophy in 1951, the same year Chris Argyris began his tenure at Yale as a professor. Schön went on to Harvard to earn his Ph.D. in philosophy with a dissertation on John Dewey's method of inquiry. Schön provided the philosophical grounding and the clout of pragmatism for the development of organizational learning, while Argyris furnished the organizational and psychological perspective.

The rationale for organizational learning emerged from Schön's influential book *Beyond the Stable State: Public and Private Learning in a Changing Society* (1973). The thesis of this book is that change is now the only constant in modern life and that we must develop social systems to cope with the change by constantly learning to adapt. Schön (1973) puts it this way:

> The loss of the stable state means that our society and all of its institutions are in continuing processes of transformation. We cannot expect new stable states that will endure even for our lifetimes. We must learn to understand, guide, influence and manage these transformations. We must make the capacity for understanding them integral to ourselves and to our institutions. We must, in other words, become adept at learning. We must become able not only to transform our institutions, in response to changing situations and requirement; we must invent and develop institutions which are 'learning systems,' that is to say systems capable of bringing about their own continuing transformation. The task, which the loss of the stable state makes imperative, for the person, for our institution, for our society as a whole, is to learn about learning. (p. 30)

This statement is a simple yet profound acknowledgement of how change is accelerating; hence the need for greater flexibility and adaptation under girds the rationale for continual and organizational learning.

What is remarkable about these thoughts is that they were written more than 30 years ago, before the personal computer and information technology engrossed everyday life. Schön's philosophical thesis provided the tenets for why organizational learning is a reasonable and necessary approach to societal issues of contemporary life. Action research, which was started by Lewin, is a moderate response to Marx's critique that "philosophers have interpreted the world in many ways, the point is to change it." Schön uses pragmatism to move past the epistemological perseveration and endless analysis, with the corroboration of Kuhn (1970) and Polanyi (1958), toward a philosophy that addresses the contemporary social issues facing humankind. At the same time Schön stresses the importance of reflection, a think-on-your-feet approach that is present in professions (e.g., physicians, attorneys, managers) as a means for learning on the job (Schön 1983, 1987).

When performing highly specialized tasks like surgery or interpreting legal texts, professionals must draw on tacit knowledge, also called "know–how," to perform at a professional standard. Tacit knowledge is not imparted from explicit sources such as books or lectures. There is an intuitive nature that is not reducible to "know-that" type of knowledge. For instance, native speakers know grammar at a tacit level, and if asked to explain a grammatical rule, many would be speechless because that knowledge is used primarily at a tacit level.

Similarly, jazz musicians improvise by intuition, at a tacit level, rather than by music theory or a set of rules. Knowing music theory helps. However, classically trained musicians' interpretation normally comes from sheet music rather than joining in on a riff or melody played by other musicians. Jazz musicians learn to improvise and gain mastery from reflection on what they have played and what other musicians have played in the past. Max De Pree (1993) drew on this jazz metaphor in his book *Leadership Jazz* to explain how leaders must listen and reflect on what others are saying and be able to improvise and accompany others' performance. Schön, in fact, was an accomplished musician who played piano and clarinet in jazz bands and chamber music as an avocation, having studied music at the Sorbonne and Conservatoire Nationale de Music in Paris (Smith, 2003b).

The theme of reflection and *The Reflective Practitioner* (1983) represent the central academic contribution of Schön. There is a clear connection between reflection on action and what may be learned from that event and the practitioner's actions and reflections. Dewey's ideas of inquiry and learning are the likely sources of Schön's reflective learning. The five phases of reflective learning are: 1) suggestions, the first idea that comes to mind toward possible solutions; 2) transformation of an intellectual perplexity into a problem to be solved; 3) use of suggestions as hypotheses to guide observation and data collection; 4) mental elaboration of the idea or supposition (thinking through possible solutions); and 5) testing the hypothesis by action (Dewey, 1933, pp. 106-116). These aspects of reflective thought are suggested as a means to learning. As a student of Dewey, Schön elaborates and updates these concepts for the purpose of organizational learning.

System Thinking

The works of Arygris and Schön are built on the premise that organizations are best understood as a system. Under the framework of this literature review, system theory is considered under a modernist rubric. Science and engineering consider system theory as the quintessential model to explain and understand dynamic phenomena. Boulding's (1956) hierarchy of systems posits that social organizations are one of the most complex systems in this hierarchy. Also known as an open-system model, this scientific model affected the study of organizations and is exemplified in the works of Bateson (1972), Beer (1979), Emery (1969), and Katz & Kahn (1978).

During the same time that system thinking was pervading studies of organizations, a philosophical revolution was questioning the scientific premises of positivism in the 1950s and empiricism in the 1960s in the so-called hard sciences. Even today among chemists and biologists, there is little acknowledgment of this revolution. The complex revolution may be summarized by the often-quoted words of N. R. Hanson: "All data are theory laden" (cited in Barbour 1974, p. 95). In other words, data are generated with a hypothesis to prove or disprove. The interpretation of the research is in play before the data are evident. The preponderance of the research is extrapolated convincingly in the work of Hanson (1958), Kuhn (1970), Polanyi (1958) and Toulmin (1960) leaving no uninterpreted data. A similar theme was explored by Schön in his earliest work, The Displacement of Concepts (1967/1963), which compares models and metaphors. Schön describes in detail models and metaphors that serve as methods to explore new situations.

In the narrative of ideas of organizational learning a shift toward *An Interpretative Turn* was taking place. Hiley, Bohman, & Shusterman (1991) compiled a set of essays from Thomas Kuhn, Richard Rorty, Charles Taylor, and others that argue differences of interpretation in the natural sciences and the human sciences. Taylor, for example, saw marked differences between the study of the human genome and human behavior. Rorty argued that both types of science were more similar than different, and that inquiry is subject to the vagaries of human knowledge. Kuhn straddles a middle position, acknowledging the reasonableness of both positions.

The lesson here for organizational learning is that early innovators of organization learning studies were not essentialists. By essentialism, I refer to the idea that definitive ontological structures are discoverable and reducible to an agreed-upon description. Many intellectual skirmishes can be traced to a search for some "true essence" of a learning organization and whether any essence actually exists. For instance, early debate centered on which units or levels of analysis were most appropriate. Is organizational learning merely the sum total of individual learning or is there a collective nature to learning? March and Olsen (1975) argued the former position and took a more empiricist position that human attributes should not be reified (Easterby-Smith, Crossan & Nicolini, 2000). Others have taken the position that learning can abide in organizational structures, traditions, and procedures and culture that affect individual learning (Fiol & Lyles, 1985).

The cognitive and behavioral debate is another example of an essentialist debate related to which object of analysis is most apt. In this debate, Learning is considered cognitive, whereas behavior is considered adaptive. Fiol and Lyles (1985) reviewed 15 papers that argued different combinations of this cognitive/behavior distinction. This debate has since become dormant, with new debates taking its place. During this period, there was a proliferation of articles that minimize the pragmatic and action-oriented roots of organizational learning. This debate on the so-called essential nature of learning within organizations ran it course and new ideas emerged.

During the late 1980s and early 1990s, an explosion of literature on organizational learning emerged, mostly within the modernist paradigm. The popularization of organizational learning was due in large part to Peter Senge (1990), who wrote *The Fifth Discipline: The Art and Practice of the Learning Organization*, noted by *Harvard Business Review* (1997) as one of two of the most important business books written in the 1990s. In a 1998 interview Senge reflected on the publication of *The Fifth Discipline*:

> All of this resulted from the simple vision that I did want to put a stake in the ground for organizational learning. The hundreds of thousands of copies that have sold were a complete surprise. I'm not even sure that it's such a good idea for the field that this book has been as popular as it has. (Fulmer & Keys, p. 34)

Since 1990, hundreds of books, dissertations, and articles (e.g., Crossan, 1999; Gravin, 1993; Huber, 1991; Levitt & March, 1988; March, 1991; Nonaka, 1991;

Nonaka & Takeuchi, 1995; Redding & Catalanello, 1994; Walkins & Marsick, 1993; Weick & Westley, 1994) have been published espousing the virtues and benefits of learning organizations. Yet in spite of this flurry of publishing activity, few authors have synthesized the existing literature, with one recent notable exception.

DiBella and Nevis

In 1998, two M.I.T. researchers, DiBella and Nevis, published How Organizations Learn. Along with grounding their theory in research, they provide several useful distinctions and a schema that provides a means to classify different perspectives on organizational learning. For example, a helpful distinction is made between the terms "learning organization" and "organizational learning." Often in the literature these terms are interchangeably used. However, DiBella and Nevis point out that a learning organization is an ideal, an abstract conceptual construct, whereas organizational learning is comprised of activities that can be observed and described in every organization.

Moreover, DiBella and Nevis (1998) submit that there are three different perspectives on how organizations learn. These differences are noted in order to discern the strengths of each perspective and then each perspective is reintegrated into a theoretical framework. One is the capability perspective, which holds that all organizations have an innate capability to learn. The obvious questions are: What does an organization learn? And how does it learn? Within the capability perspective it is understood that the lessons organizations learn may not prove beneficial to the organization's goals. For instance, Argyris (1992) wrote about "skilled incompetence" and "defensive routines." There is also the idea of unlearning in the organization (McGill & Slocum, 1993) before beneficial learning will take place. Scholars and practitioners who share the capability perspective include Jelinek (1979), Stata (1989), and Wenger (1996). Moreover, Wenger (1998) further developed a theory of learning that begins with the assumption that social participation is the main way that people learn. These informal "communities of practice" comprise the relationships that people form to accomplish tasks.

The second distinction DiBella and Nevis (1998) note is the developmental perspective, which assumes the capability perspective, yet stresses that organizations learn as a result of experience over time. Organizations attain the distinction as learning organizations through stages of development. Development may be the result of evolutionary or revolutionary factors or both. An organization also may develop as a result of size, age, industry change, and organizational life cycle (Greiner, 1972; Handy, 1993). Evolutionary factors are the gradual changes that occur from small adjustments as an organization changes. Revolutionary change could be industry-specific changes in products or environmental economic shifts during which an organization must change or pass away. In either case, learning comes from experience over time and "the learning organization may be considered the most advanced stage in any organization's development" (DiBella & Nevis, 1998, p. 11). Thus, the developmental perspective perceives organizations that have maximized their agility to a rapidly changing environment as being more developed. Adaptability, not age, is the hallmark of a learning organization. Noteworthy scholars who share the developmental perspective are Argyris and Schön (1978), Dechant and Marsick (1991), Greiner (1972), and Kimberly and Miles (1980).

The third perspective mentioned by DiBella and Nevis (1998) is the normative approach, which implies that unless certain conditions (e.g., norms) are met or overcome, organizational learning will not occur. Senge (1990) suggests that five disciplines contribute to organizational learning: personal mastery, mental models, shared vision, team learning, and system thinking; all are influenced predominately by the normative perspective.

The advantage of the DiBella and Nevis's (1998) work is that it organizes and integrates the three perspectives in a way that shows the strengths of each of the positions noted above. The limitation of each perspective is compensated for by a clarification of what each perspective does and does not do. In essence, DiBella and Nevis (1998) took a rapidly emerging field of organizational learning, with dozens of authors and their compelling points of views, and classified the reflections of both scholars and practitioners so these ideas may be understood, compared and used to enhance the actual practice of organizational learning.

Besides clarifying integrating organizational learning theory, DiBella and Nevis (1998) developed an instrument for indicating some tendencies for how an organization learns. I planned to use this Organizational Learning Profile (OLP) to check the agreement between how employees perceived the learning at Delta Technologies, but my request to have each employee fill out the OLP at an all-staff meeting was denied. After I was denied permission, I decided to forgo any significant use of the OLP. My only use of the OLP was limited to add structure and a platform during half the interviews.

The work of DiBella and Nevis (1998) exemplifies and summarizes the best of the modern organizational theory paradigm. It integrates and applies dispersed ideas of organizational learning to practical business problems. One reason DiBella and Nevis (1998) were able to transcend the paradigmatic quandary is that they had pragmatic goals: to put knowledge into action and assist organizations to change. Another reason for the orderliness of their integrated approach was that interpretative and critical paradigms were not addressed. Rather, each modern theory has a function and DiBella and Nevis (1998) described these functions within their framework. It was classic theorist Max Weber (1864-1920) who first saw societal and organizational groups in functionalist terms. (Weber's analysis was much more nuance than this simple depiction.) The main reason DiBella and Nevis's integrated approach works is that it stresses synthesis, homogeneity, and coherence, all of which are emphasized at the expense of disjunction, ambiguity, and difference. The functional theme of order in organizations and society is the hallmark of modernity. However, Weber cannot be accused of dichotomous thinking. Weber uses the German word *verstehen*, translated as "understanding;" this language suggests an attempt to interpret meaning of a situation from the actors perspective rather than from a reductionistic functional analysis. In other words, the seeds of interpretative analysis were latent in Weber's functionalism. We turn now from Max Weber's ideas to G.W. Mead's ideas as the founder of interpretative organizational analysis or, in his parlance, symbolic interactionism.

Interpretative Paradigms

The first example of a scholar on the cusp between modernism and interpretivism is Edgar Schein. Writing for a business audience, Schein makes a case for understanding and "managing" organizational cultures. Organizational cultures are defined as "shared norms, values, and assumptions" (Schein, 1992, p. 229). According to Schein, the culture of an organization can be managed into a learning organization by competent leadership (Schein, 1992, pp. 361-392). However, previously Smircich and Calás (1987) took exception to the notion that culture is something that can be managed or intentionally changed. Rather, they assert that jumping on the organizational cultural bandwagon and attempting to control organizational culture will likely result in draining the culture of its vitality. There are multiple values active in organizations and attempting to portray or manipulate those different values will result in pushing minority values underground. Smircich and Calás (1987) wrote:

The phrase "organizational culture" in corporate culture literature is often used as a "cookie cutter" placed on the whole fabric of belief systems that pervade organizational life. The corporate culture perspective cuts and delimits the range of shared understandings that receive attention from researchers. For example, corporate culture researchers rarely discuss the subcultures of management, shared understanding that unite[s] people on the basis of power and class. (p. 239)

Doing a cultural analysis of an organization is not to discover a silver bullet to fix a business's problem, but to provide an understanding about an organization's unique culture. The corporate culture perspective that Smircich and Calás (1987) berated came from an article in Business Week entitled "Corporate Culture." The move to commodify and justify every organizational endeavor in terms of a "return on investment" appears nearly endless. If we cannot see past the packaging, then our learning lacks the depth and critical thinking we need to guide us.

Schein (1992) introduced the concepts of organizational culture and learning so that a business audience could appreciate how misunderstanding cultural differences could hinder organizational effectiveness. More specifically, Schein (1996) argues that within organizations there exist sub-cultures, such as executive and engineering levels, that fail to understand each other and therefore fail to learn. Schein's intrepretivism is useful, but rather predictable and staid.

Another example of a scholar who addressed organizational learning and culture is Karl Weick. As a social psychologist, Weick's training encompassed both learning from numerous psychological perspectives (e.g., behavioral, humanist, cognitive, and social) and examining organizational behavior from distinct sociological outlooks. His cross-disciplinary approach surveyed what various academic camps were espousing. Weick's early works appear almost positivistic in that his system approach, with organizational dynamic mapped out with great detail in flow charts (e.g., The Social Psychology of Organizing, 1979). Later Weick's (1995) enactment theory and sense-making developed into a more interpretative and constructivist approach.

Weick's premise is that in highly complex, uncertain environments people attempt to make sense and organize in the face of that uncertainty. Weick

(1979b) suggests that people engage in "equivocality-reduction" in order to explain or make sense of organizational ambiguity by interpreting circumstances in various ways. Draft and Weick (1984) compare four models of interpretation as systems. According to Crossan and Guatto (1996, p. 110), Draft and Weick's (1984) article was the most widely cited in organizational learning articles based on their survey of the literature. Connecting "interpretation systems" with organizational behavior gave theoretical clout to the idea of organizational learning. Moreover, Draft and Weick's piece of theorizing crosses the reified boundaries of this literature review from a modern/systems approach toward a symbolic/interpretative approach of organizations. The concept of an "interpretation system" holds two ideas together that could be consider antithetical.

Weick (1991) began to explore directly the landscape of organizational learning shortly after Senge (1990) published his popular bestseller. It was also during the late 1980s and early 1990s that ideas were being posited with little attention to what other scholars were putting forward. Geertz (1973) refers to this phenomenon as collective autism. Weick (1991) alleges that organizational learning conflates change, learning, and adaptation. To untangle these ideas Weick considered a "traditional psychological definition of learning," by which he meant a stimulus-response of behaviorism. He concluded that organizational learning is nontraditional in its approach to learning and more closely resembles sensemaking.

In Weick's (1995) *Sensemaking in Organizations*, the preface starts with "This book is written as if Lave and Wenger's (1991) concept of 'legitimate peripheral participation' was a valid portrait as a cognitive apprenticeship" (p. xi). Later in this chapter the theories of both Lave & Wenger (1991) and Wenger (1998) will be considered as the most practical and theoretically rigorous means to understanding organizational learning. It is noteworthy that Weick saw the interpretative connections of situated learning and sensemaking with organizational learning.

Perhaps Weick's most insightful essay on organizational learning is playfully entitled "Organizational Learning: Affirming the Oxymoron" (Weick & Westley, 1996). Here the nontraditional and the paradoxical attributes of organizational learning are embraced and explained. Weick and Westley argue that organizing and learning are essentially antithetical processes. To learn is to disorganize and increase variety. To organize is to forget and reduce variety. In the rush to embrace learning, organizational theorists often overlook this tension, which explains why they are never sure whether learning is something new or simply warmed-over organizational change (p. 440).

Weick and Westley explore the circumstances in which moments of learning take place. For example, reflection (e.g., Schön, 1983) must take place, and standard operating procedures need to be questioned so that doubt and curiosity are cultivated (1996, p. 444). Rather than agree with March's (1991) distinction that "self-designing organizations have the tendency to explore [to learn], bureaucracies to exploit," Weick & Westley (1996, p. 445) suggest that all organizations are better off to engage in both exploring and exploiting for learning to occur.

What Weick & Westley (1996) strive to do is to bring together distinctions that are part of the organizational paradox called organizational learning. For instance, some (Ackoff, 1994; March & Olsen, 1975; Schein, 1996; Simon, 1991) have argued that organizational learning is merely the sum total of individual learning and are concerned that we might be attributing human characteristics like "learning" to inanimate objects like organizations. Other theorists have argued that organizational learning is more than the sum of its parts. Fiol & Lyles (1985) allege that organizational systems, procedures, and social structures affect the learning of individuals in that organization. Moreover, others further suggest that learning is stored in the systems, procedures, and social structures of organizations (Hedberg,1981;Shrivastava, 1983). Hedberg summarizes this point:

...although organizational learning occurs through individuals, it would be a mistake to conclude that organizational learning is nothing but the cumulative result of the members' learning. Members come and go, and leadership changes, but organizations' memories preserve certain behaviors, mental maps, norms and values over time. (1981, p. 6, cited in Easterby-Smith, Crossan, & Nicolini, 2000, p. 785)

Weick and Westley (1996) considered learning so important that they do not split the issues of individual learning and social learning. It is not an either/or issue, but a both/and issue (Kim, 1993). Weick and Westley (1996) urge the reader to set aside this either/or squabble, saying, "We must proceed with the faith that social learning processes have something to teach us about individual learning, as well as vice versa" (p. 442). It is fascinating that these hard-nosed social scientists appealed to their colleagues to have "faith" to set aside this minor dispute, because at the heart of the matter, language is inadequate to explain a phenomenon that is paradoxical. Similarly, Schwandt (1994) uses the word "persuasions" to describe the interpretative positions.

Because we are dealing with events that are situated or contextual by their nature, learning in organizations is understood best when organizations are seen as cultures with artifacts, language, and values that provide a context or situation infused with meaning to be interpreted. Weick and Westley make the "organization as a culture argument" as a means of embracing all elements that are simultaneously taking place. All those elements or, as Weick and Westley put it, "learning moments," can play off each other. One culture specific trait, for example, is humor. In the research for this dissertation humor played a significant theme. The idea of an organization as a culture, or a tribe, or a community will be explored in greater detail in Chapter Three.

Weick and Westley (1996) are exemplars of the movement from a modernist paradigm toward an interpretative/symbolic paradigm of organization studies. To delineate the importance and ramifications of an interpretative perspective to organization theory could result in an entirely separate book. It is a massive topic, with a multifaceted, far-flung confluence of ideas that lead to different interpretative approaches. For example, interpretative approaches could be traced back decades to the philosophical roots in the discipline of hermeneutics (Grondin, 1995). For this particular study, however, the number of scholars who embrace both interpretivism and constructivism along with organizational learning is limited. Nevertheless, since the interpretative perspectives share an epistemological skepticism questioning empirical positivism's claims to see and discover the essential nature of things, explaining some of the philosophic roots of intrepretivism and constructivism helps explain why intrepretivism was selected as part of this project. For the sake of brevity, the following explanation will include the elements that interpretivism and constructivism share. Schwandt (1994) marks the difference between the two while acknowledging "the risk of drawing too fine a distinction" (p. 119). To avoid this risk, when I refer to interpretivism, I intend to include constructivism. The risk mentioned above was noted by William of Ockham (1285-1349) as the "principle of parsimony," or Ockham's razor, which holds that the explanation that requires the fewest assumptions is preferred. In other words, distinctions that do not make a difference are to be avoided.

Interpretivism emerged in reaction to the modern, rationalistic assumption that reality could be broken down to its smallest parts and that its essential nature is discoverable. Interpretivism maintains that knowledge is partial, tentative, and provisional. The process of interpretation includes the construal of meaning, and therefore constructivism is integral to the interpretative process. Meanings are socially constructed and socially shared (Berger & Luckman, 1966). Recognizing the extent and magnitude of the socialization process may result in a person becoming humble and flexible in their relations with others. Of course, there is no simplistic cause and effect link that results in a socially gracious individual. Still, the quality of social relations depends on people sharing some degree of common ground. Even a shared recognition of particular forces of socialization that shape and limit a person's formation does not provide the common ground guaranteeing that a person will be less dogmatic about their beliefs. Nevertheless, interpretivism suggests the visceral knowledge of our socialization process has the potential for our limited perspective to be a common ground for understanding.

Interpretivism also holds that events or texts will have more than one equally valid interpretation. There is not one definitive interpretation of anything, according to an interpretative perspective, since people bring their situated self into each hermeneutical circle. In his book Available Light (Geertz, 2000) refers to the experiences and perspectives that we bring to each event or text. We do not see directly, but rather "as" a certain person with a given history, replete with assumptions and values.

Star (1991) referred to the interpretative endeavor as articulation work. Words are chosen with great care to convey what the researcher wishes to convey. Events are considered a text to be pondered and understood (Geertz, 1973). It is not accidental that the interpretative practice is considered "persuasion" (Schwandt, 1994). Interpretivism is indeed philosophical persuasion that cannot be proven, as if anything can be proven. It is a position that has been assumed as a result of reflection on a preponderance of experience and evidentiary arguments.

Truth found in interpretative research is akin to truth found in a novel or a film, whereas truth found in a lab experiment or in a statistical regression is acceptance or rejection of a null hypothesis, a predetermined measurement of a certain condition or treatment. Interpretative research narrates stories (Banks & Banks, 1998; Burns-McCoy, 1998; Morris, 2000; Wenger, 1990) to evoke and enliven the truths found and explained. At times fiction can be used to tell the story, with the caveat that the way the fiction is used in the interpretation is made explicit.

Those who share this interpretative paradigm question or are critical of any knowledge claims that are taken for granted (Burr, 1995). Arguments using categories, such as liberal or conservative, for instance, have contextual meanings. These categories are perceived to exist, yet these are not actual categories but interpretation of points of view. If one compares a newspaper from Europe to a newspaper from the United States, one will likely see very different positions in the categories of liberal and conservative. Categories are social constructions that are situated, and therefore are taken for granted with agreed upon characteristics by a social group. Even categories with scientific nomenclature, such as mammals and reptiles, still are socially constructed from physiological functions of certain creatures, albeit there is agreement between members of scientific communities of what characteristics fit in which category (Latour & Woolgar, 1979). The very idea of "agreed upon characteristics" intimates what social constructivists argue—that social groups construe knowledge and ideas. Bowker and Star (1999) argue that classification is found in almost every area of our lives:

> Remarkably for such a central part of our lives, we stand for the most part in formal ignorance of the social and moral order created by these invisible, potent entities. Their impact is indisputable, and as Foucault reminds us, inescapable. Try the simple experiment of ignoring your gender classification and use instead whichever toilets are the nearest; try and locate a library book shelved under the wrong Library of Congress catalogue number; stand in the immigration queue at a busy foreign airport without the right passport or arrive without the transformer and adapter that translates between electrical standards. The material force of categories appears always and instantly. (p. 3)

Our knowledge comes to us embedded in a social and historical context, replete with categories. It is difficult, if not impossible, to understand knowledge apart from understanding the context from which it was constructed. Interpretivism contends that our knowledge is never free from contextual and historical influences. For example, 80 years ago those who drank alcoholic beverages to excess were considered morally flawed. Now, those with similar behavioral characteristics likely are considered to be afflicted with the disease of alcoholism (Denzin & Johnson, 1993). Interpretivists merely want to point out that knowledge generation does not occur in a vacuum, but in a context bristling with assumptions. Moreover, social processes also allegedly maintain knowledge.

Beliefs, for example, are maintained by plausibility structures in religious communities (Berger, 1990). Gathering together for worship and prayer helps sustain shared beliefs. The meanings of beliefs are negotiated, which also encourages shared community knowledge. In addition, social processes involve action, and it is action or practice that also aids social construction and interpretation. Dawson (1967) suggested that Christianity and Islam grew and endured because ritual and liturgy were practiced. Social practice, perhaps more than anything, has solidified communities during difficult times.

The reason these social dynamics are mentioned in this literature review is that organizational learning is social by definition. This social learning assertion will be fortified when communities of practice and social learning are explored in the pages ahead. To summarize thus far, there are important philosophical distinctions between interpretivists and modernist (i.e., reductionist) scholars in organizational learning. First, among rationalistic and reductionistic scholars there appears to be an assumption that people are seen as distinct from the world. Sandberg (2000) described this meta-theory as "a dualistic ontology, assuming that person and world exist as distinct entities, and an objectivistic epistemology, assuming the existence of an objective reality independent of and beyond the human mind" (p. 11). Sandberg (2000) refers to numerous authors who have elaborated on the troublesome ramification of this dualistic assertion (Bernstein, 1983; Husserl, 1970/1936; Rorty, 1979; Schön, 1983; Searle, 1992; Shotter, 1992; Winograd & Flores, 1986).

The interpretative tradition suggests that humans are ineluctably linked to the context in which they are living. The assumption here is that distinctions between components are mutually constituted. Separating elements from a context as more or less important misses the entirety of the phenomenon.

When organizational learning theory first began to emerge it was understandable that an interpretative framework was not a means of investigation. Interpretative and qualitative research was, and in some circles still is, relegated to second-class status. Organizational learning sprang from a pragmatic, modern, business-oriented approach within a behavioral, positivistic framework, in spite of Schön's (1983, 1987) philosophical erudition. It was the wave of pragmatics in education and learning, along with system thinking (Senge, 1990), that influenced the formation of organizational learning. Interpretivism was not seen as beneficial and advantageous to organizational learning. It was the emergence of critical thought in organizational studies that made interpretative research more perceptive in organizational learning investigations. Friendly critics introduced interpretative research into the organizational learning literature (Schein 1992; Weick, 1995; Weick & Westley, 1996).

However, when learning is a goal, criticism need not be merely negative. Rather there is a salutary outcome in the long run. This will be evidenced as this chapter concludes with an explanation of communities of practice. It is my conviction that community of practice is an organic progeny of organizational learning. I will argue that the communities of practice theory are developing with an identification of our knowledge limitations, unrecognized in some earlier forms of organizational learning.

Communities of Practice

Not surprisingly, it was a community of researchers who first coined the term communities of practice. The roots of communities of practice reach back to the late 1970s to the Xerox Palo Alto Research Center (PARC), where anthropologists and computer scientists worked together to understand everyday use and practice of technology (Suchman, Bloomberg, Orr & Trigg, 1999).[2]

Later the Xerox Foundation formed the Institute for Research on Learning (IRL), also in Palo Alto, California, to explore the practice of learning. The

---

[2] see http://www.parc.xerox.com/company/history/

charter of IRL came from a national report to study learning, A Nation at Risk (http://www.ed.gov/pubs/NatAtRisk/risk.html). Since learning was considered such a crucial issue, it was studied by several disciplines so that no single discipline would "own" learning. Communities of practice became the terminology to embrace different viewpoints of cultural anthropologists, cogitative psychologists, educators, and computer scientists to explore a broader understanding of learning. Rather than looking at learning in the traditional classroom setting, researchers at IRL looked at informal learning and apprenticeship in the workplace.

For instance, Orr's (1996) ethnographic study of photocopy machine repair technicians and their methods of learning exemplified a situated approach to learning (Brown & Duguid, 1991). Orr observed there were canonical methods of repairing a photocopy machine by following the book and then there were non-canonical methods that practitioners preferred, such as talking shop over coffee or a meal (Orr, 1996). It was not only that the non-canonical method was preferred, it appeared that that learning and practice advanced in a more organic way. Put another way, a community of practice is a "living curriculum" (Wenger, 2003), much more able to grow and change in our information-driven world.

The term communities of practice emerged first in print during the collaboration of Lave and Wenger in writing Situated Learning: Legitimate Peripheral Participation (1991). Lave is a professor of education and served as a member of Wenger's dissertation committee. Wenger then was a computer science Ph.D. candidate specializing in artificial intelligence. Wenger (1987, 1989) had published works on artificial intelligence and tutoring systems and found that technology often overlooked the human dimensions such as meaning and identity in understanding learning systems. It was the ambitious goal in Situated Learning to shift the focus of learning from the individual to the whole person, where activity, agent and context are seen as mutually constitutive.

Lave and Wenger (1991) considered apprenticeships in five different situations: Yucatec midwives, Vai and Gola tailors, naval quartermasters, meat cutters, and non-drinking alcoholics. In each case:

> Learning viewed as a situated activity has as its central defining characteristic a process that we call legitimate peripheral participation. By this we mean to draw attention to the point that learners inevitably participate in communities of practitioners and that the mastery of knowledge and skill requires newcomers to move toward full participation in the sociocultural practice of a community. "Legitimate peripheral participation" provides a way to speak about the relations between newcomers and old-timers, about activities, identities, artifacts, and communities of knowledge and practice. (p. 29)

Clearly, learning is considered social in nature as opposed to the traditionally narrow focus on behavioral or cognitive paradigms of learning. More specifically, according to Lave and Wenger, learning is located in the practice or co-participation between members of a community rather than merely sequestered in the heads of individuals. The community focus of learning provides organizational learning social units of understanding to explore, analyze, and enhance learning. Lave and Wenger's research colleagues at The Institute for Research on Learning likewise elaborate on the social dimensions of learning (Brown & Duguid, 1991), pushing the social learning theories of Bandura (1977, 1986), Rogoff & Wertsch (1984), and Vygotsky (1978) by placing learning into the broader field of social theory.

More recently, Wenger (1998) precisely develops a theory of social learning within social theory by drawing on the multiple theories that contribute to our understanding of learning. Again, learning is a topic too broad and human in our information-driven world to be relegated to one academic discipline like education or psychology. Wenger (1998) summarizes with post-modern sensibilities thus:

> The purpose of this book is not to propose a grandiose synthesis of these intellectual traditions or a resolution of the debates they

reflect; my goal is much more modest. Nonetheless, that each of these traditions has something crucial to contribute to what I call a social theory of learning is in itself interesting. It shows that developing such a theory comes close to developing a learning-based theory of social order. In other words, learning is so fundamental to the social order we live by that theorizing about one is tantamount to theorizing about the other. (p. 15)

The integral nature of this social theory of learning is evident in the rich theoretical streams that feed into Wenger's treatise. Yet rather than delineate each intellectual tradition at this point of this literature review, I will suggest some philosophical points in regard to a social theory of learning. The theoretical contribution from numerous theories remains for further exploration. However, I reiterate my conviction that pragmatism will be the most fruitful avenue of exploration of Wenger's theory of social learning as it is applied to actual situations and further theoretical considerations.

Pragmatists such as Richard Rorty (1979), Cornel West (1989), and especially John Dewey (1859-1952) provided the philosophical clout and flexibility to interpret social theories that inform communities of practice. It was Dewey's social epistemology centering on action and practice that provided the rationale for the ideas behind social learning. Although Dewey is mentioned little in Wenger's social learning theory, Dewey eschewed analytical philosophy and its priority of conceptual representations and essentialism that claims it understands the "true" nature of things or events. As a result, a need for an epistemology of social contructionism was required. Pragmatism provides a comprehension of why a social construction of knowledge makes sense as we act in the world with limited and parochial knowledge claims. Explaining how things actually are differs from explaining how things appear to work. Conflating these two explorations is often deleterious to our practice.

Contemporary social constructivist epistemology will be advanced if we better understand Dewey's contribution to educational philosophy. For instance, Dewey pointed out the importance of language in practice. In reference to language Dewey (1925/1981) wrote, "As to be a tool, or to be used as means for consequences, is to have and to endow with meaning, language, being the tool of tools is the cherishing mother of all significance" (p. 146, cited in Garrison, 1995, p. 721). A contemporary example of the importance of language to social theory is in Wenger (1998), as practice and reification is negotiated and shared meaning is the result. Knowledge is seen as constructed in a social process.

Dewey's method of inquiry rejected scientific realism. As an alternative to realism, Dewey suggested instrumentalism or productive pragmatism. Facts were not considered as true in and of themselves, but only as means to advance further inquiry. In other words, facts are facts-in-a-case (Hickman, 2001), or facts are situated in a given context. Researchers at IRL Brown, Collins, and Duguid (1989) overlook that Dewey had already provided at least a prologue for social epistemology for learning and inquiry when they concluded that "the unheralded importance of activity and enculturation to learning suggests that much common education practice is victim of an inadequate epistemology. A new epistemology might hold the key to a dramatic improvement in learning and a completely new perspective on education" (p. 41). The new epistemology that Brown et. al. (1989) advocated is a situated cognition where a constructivist epistemology can make sense of learning within a practice. It was Lave and Wenger (1991) who pushed social learning even further and suggested the social construction of knowledge situated within a practice, and it is where newcomers move from the periphery of a practice into the center. However, it was Dewey (1933) who first suggested a more adequate epistemology of learning and inquiry and thereby provided some of the philosophical underpinning.

To conclude this section I will introduce some key aspects of Wenger's social theory of learning. Communities of practice can be defined as " groups of people who share a concern, a set of problems, or a passion about a topic, and who deepen their knowledge and expertise in this area by interacting on an ongoing basis" (Wenger, McDermott & Snyder, 2002, p. 4). Communities of practice can form intentionally, but often form spontaneously from a shared passion; they can be large or small; they can form in one location or be distributed across the globe over the Internet.

Communities of practice share three elements that will help define the shared dynamics of a particular community, namely: domain, community, and practice. First, communities of practice share a domain of knowledge. This shared knowledge base guides the members as to how a practice is carried out and what is the cutting edge so members might advance their collective knowledge. It is this shared commitment to advancing the practice, knowing what is important or trivial, that constitutes the domain.

Second, communities weave a social fabric for learning. Ideally, there is a positive regard for each other and a safe place to ask questions, show ignorance, and make mistakes. Here the novice is "shown the ropes" and is able to learn "shoulder to shoulder." As novices are legitimized and move from the periphery toward the center of the practice, novices become apprentices, and in turn share their experience with fresh novices. Newcomers also end up contributing to the evolution of the practice. Learning is much more a matter of belonging than a matter of knowing. Without genuine acceptance into a social group, learning becomes devoid of human qualities such as making sense of our existence.

Third, practice refers to the actual behavior in which members engage while conducting tasks. One could think of a medical doctor performing an examination or an attorney asking questions during a deposition. The connotation of practice here is socially agreed upon performance. As Wenger et. al. (2002, p. 38) state, practice is defined as "a set of common approaches and shared standards that create a basis for action, communication, problem solving, performance, and accountability." Taken together, these elements of community, domain, and practice provide a framework to understand the basic functions of a community of practice.

I turn now to consider how literary patterns in the domains of organizational learning and communities of practice play out in light critical organizational theory, especially in light organizational analysis.

The Disputed Terrain of Post-Modern Organizational Analysis

Surveys of sociological paradigms of organizational analysis (Burrell & Morgan, 1979) provide insights into what is available for organizational analysis, but are in scarce agreement about the referential standard of analysis. Not since Weber's functionalism has any consensus between organizational researchers on which paradigm, metaphor, or concept should be considered as a standard method organizational analysis (Burrell, 1996). Burrell argues that the most appropriate metaphor to explain the major impasse in the organizational analysis community of scholars is that of the biblical myth of the Tower of Babel (p. 645). The builders, who endeavor to reach the heavens with their tower, before long are unable to understand each other. Burrell's allusion to a tower that reaches to the heavens is suggestive of Foucault's (1977) criticism of panopticon (vision over all, a type of divine omniscience). Foucault's direct allusion here is a prison camera that is able to view the inmate's life at all times, which is reminiscent of Weber's (1947, in Hatch, 1997, p. 33) "iron cage" of bureaucracy. Conceptualization in organization theory operates as a means to sequester an organization for examination and dissection. Burrell (1996) elaborates what concepts are capable of:

> Concepts are the ultimate form of the panopticon (Foucault, 1977). By classifying and marking their victims, concepts perform an imprisoning act of considerable sophistication. But much more than incarceration takes place. Once immobilized, the body of thought becomes subject to inscription. Concepts inscribe their marks upon the body of literature and, in the process marking with cuts and incisions, they leave a trail of lesions behind which all can follow. The deeper cuts are those which make the biggest impression upon those that read off significance of the author's (re)marks for themselves. But these impressive cuts ultimately spell death and immobility. At the very least the subject is wounded by the deepest and most incisive inscription. Paradigm, metaphors, discourse and genealogies are all incised lesions on the body of organizational life. Analysis of almost any kind requires the death or at least the mutilation of that which is analyzed. (p. 645)

Elsewhere in the same essay, Burrell states that "science begins by placing the perpetually dynamic into a field of stasis." He goes on to cite an example of "a 4,900-year-old bristle cone pine in Wyoming cut down by an impatient researcher because his tree corer would not work. The oldest living thing on the planet was killed in order to find out how old it was" (Zwicky, 1992, cited in Burrell, 1996, p. 645). The scathing critique above is only a sample of Burrell's trenchant deconstructive essay. How does one move forward in this dissertation chapter on the analysis of data in light of such a blistering reproach?

Primarily, researchers move ahead with humility and caution, under the Hippocratic oath to above all "do no harm." This requires that we acknowledge the tension created by our responsibility to do no harm and yet to explain the narrative to the best of our understanding while knowing our explanation might very well harm others. It is also incumbent on research to be explicit as to the purpose of the research. Research ethics boils down to respecting the informants and their concerns, since it is their life that is interwoven into the organization under examination (Spradley, 1980, pp. 20-25). When a patient under medical care, you know when you've been treated with care and respect. Often invasive care is necessary to understand the malady from which we are suffering. [3]

Premodern organizational forms

Burrell posits that a way forward from this postmodern quandary is toward a premodern understanding of organizations. The limit of modern rationality started with Kant and Decartes and, in many respects, postmodernism suggests that rationality has gone to seed. West (1989) argues that Foucault is asking

---

[3] There is a case to be made where organizations need to be examined and analyzed, such as the criminal activity of clergy sex abuse in the Catholic Church, or the fraud allegations against Enron, WorldCom, or Adelphia, for example. Organizations that allow children to be assaulted or investors and employees defrauded of their life savings must be analyzed in order to understand how the growths of malignancy begin. Horrendous harm has already been done.

Kantian and Cartesian questions that lead to "answers [that] shun the centrality of dynamic social practices structured and unstructured over time and space" (p. 225). Rather than focus on analysis to reach some elusive essentialism that depicts the ontology of an organization, pragmatism focuses instead on the improvement of organizational practices as a path out of a postmodern quandary. The purpose of pragmatic organizational analysis is a means to make organizations more humane and sanguine to human aspirations. Pragmatism need not become a tool for the worship of efficiency at the price of human dignity. Instead, pragmatism is a philosophical tradition that eschews ontological and epistemological focused philosophies because they have turned out to be intellectual dead ends.

William of Ockham (1285-1349), a premodern, yet critical thinker is considered one the more prominent philosophers of the 14th century and a controversial theologian. It was Ockham's adherents who derided medieval theologians with the hyperbolic criticism of analysis by claiming certain theologians would argue how many angels could fit on the head of pin. Ockham, instead, advocated what is known as the rule of parsimony, or principle of economy, otherwise known as Ockham's Razor. This rule is summed up as: "One should not increase, beyond what is necessary, the number of entities required to explain anything" (Heylighen, 1997).

Pragmatists concur, but take Ockham's Razor into the arena of practice and stress that practice is where a phenomenon is understood best. In other words reality is most accurately understood indirectly in practice. Unfortunately, much of academic philosophy has become so specialized that most often philosophers write for other philosophers. On the other hand, pragmatism, which is gaining substantial credibility in philosophy departments[4], sees the value of philosophizing in public and in practice. For example, Dewey (1933) placed great emphasis on public education to solve problems in a democratic fashion. The important issues of the day cannot be understood and debated to some resolution

---

[4] http://www.pragmatism.org/programs/grad.htm

by a population unless that population is thoughtful and able to consider multiple points of view. Learning is the essential element for a society to function in a civil manner.

Social Learning Theory

Social learning theory recognizes the inseparable nature of learning from its social setting. Social participation in a practice is where learning occurs (Lave & Wenger, 1991). Humans are natural learners and learning is an integral part of daily activity. Attempting to separate learning from living is akin to trying to separate the cardiovascular rhythm from mammals. One need only to observe young children learning a language to see innate human capacity to learn in action (Smilkstein, 2003). Learning integrates who we are and what we do (Wenger, 1998, pp. 143-183). The apprenticeship model exemplifies how the situation is coupled with learning. Consider, for example, the internship of a medical doctor. The learning occurs situated in the care and treatment of patients. The intern is known and trusted by sick and injured patients as "Doctor X" and the intern takes on that persona as well.

Apprenticeship models (Coy, 1989) are augmented and clarified in Situated Learning by Lave and Wenger (1991), where learning ensues in shared participation of the practice. The spatial model that Lave and Wenger advance is also known as Legitimate Peripheral Participation (LPP). This dynamic model pertains to novices who are welcomed into a practice and legitimized as authentic members of a practice. As the novice participates in the practice with other members, new apprentices move gradually toward greater competency in apprenticeship. An apprentice moves toward greater competency as s/he begins demonstrating techniques of the practice to those recently joining the practice. At the same time, these apprentices introduce new practices that influence the trajectory of the practice and its knowledge domain. Depending, of course, on the practice, an apprentice's contact with a master is determined by the situation and the need for guidance.

There are many gradations of competency as practitioners move to greater participation in their field. The crucial point is the legitimacy of one's membership in a community of practice. The legitimacy comes from the established members accepting the novice into the community, while at the same time the identity of the new participant is formed as his/her competency increases and his/her membership is solidified. For example, a medical doctor retains the sense of identity as a doctor even after leaving the hospital. Legitimacy provides the social acceptance necessary for cohesion to take place within the community of practitioners, for instance from supervising physicians. The acceptance, or positive regard (Rogers, 1995), provides the novice with the psychological safety and confidence to become a contributing member of a practice. Full engagement in the community of practitioners is truncated without the positive regard coming from established members.

Legitimacy also provides a vital arena for social learning to occur. The relationship between those with little power and those with experience, skills, and competencies is unequal. Legitimization renders social acceptance between unequal participants, which allows for more of a partnership than of a hierarchical relationship of master and novice.

Social Capital

Relationships within a community of practice recently have been coined as "social capital" to emphasize the importance of social fabric in how knowledge and innovation flow in organizations (Cohen & Prusak, 2001). Put more forcefully:

> We live today in a knowledge economy. The core assets of modern business enterprise lie not in buildings, machinery, and real estate, but in the intelligence, understanding, skills and experience of employees. Harnessing the capabilities and commitment of knowledge workers is, it might be argued, the

central managerial challenge of our time. (Manville & Ober, 2003, p. 48)

The simple yet profound recognition that people make up the crucial part of an organization (Brown & Solomon-Gray, 1995) strongly suggests that social issues are not necessarily a superficial topic, but one that has important ramifications for organizational health. A similar theme is espoused in *The Social Life of Information* (Brown & Duguid, 2000b), namely, if the social element of information is neglected, information becomes decontextualized and meaningless.

A recent example of where the social element of information was found lacking a context, with tragic results, can be found in the 832 page Congressional Report: *Joint Inquiry into Intelligence Community Activities before and after the Terrorist Attacks of September 11, 2001.* The summary findings of this report indicate that human intelligence operatives were found to be inadequate. When reports, both incoming and outgoing, from field offices were not accompanied by social connections, information was not recognized as legitimate, and therefore not taken seriously. And although there was a recognized threat coming from al-Qa'ida in the intelligence community after bombings in Africa, there was not the organizational agility to respond to the suspected threat. In short, information was decontextualized and therefore not actionable.

The problem noted above within the intelligence community was not an absence of social capital but rather was the downside of social capital that turned in on itself and became ossified in a bureaucratic context. Social worlds can become tightly integrated as did these groups within the intelligence community that become impervious to ideas outside the assumptions held by each social group. Similar communication or transfers of information problems are cited in the reasons for the Columbia space shuttle disaster[5]. It is unfortunately the case that we often learn more when things go awry than when things go well. The idea

---

[5] http://www.caib.us/news/report/default.html

that more lessons are learned from errors should be kept in mind in the pages ahead. It is not my intention to focus on negative aspects of Delta Technologies, but often that is where the examples of culture and learning are most conspicuous.

Peter Vaill (1996, p. 28) points out that common everyday phrases reflect that learning is often associated with painful experiences. Some examples are: "he learned his lesson" or "that was a real learning experience." Clearly, often learning has some less than pleasant connotation in our culture. However, when an organization's members become "reflective learners" (Schön, 1983), not succumbing to "organizational defenses" (Aygyris, 1992), organizations can promote learning by changing their routines from what has not worked in the past. Recently, Levin, Cross, and Abrams (2002) suggested that interpersonal trust enhances knowledge transfer (i.e., learning).

Interpersonal trust is an advantageous trait for members to share in an organization that wishes to learn. Certainly, learning can occur in context with strife and dissention. Yet in the long run, strife becomes deleterious and counterproductive to social cohesion. In essence, the context matters in social learning. Rather than examine one variable such as Levin et. al., I used ethnographic research methodologies to understand the context of Delta Technologies from observations, interviews, and documents to render an interpretation of the culture of this organization and how members appeared to learn. To fully appreciate the social learning of an organization, both the culture in which that organization exists as well as the corporate culture, makeup the grist of interpretation in the next chapter in which the data are analyzed. Therefore, original research questions found in the proposal were: What is the culture of Delta Technologies? How does Delta Technologies learn? Each question is seen as inextricably linked and influential to each other by virtue of the theory of social learning of Wenger (1998). How these questions are answered in an interpretative study could be approached any number of ways. I turn now to present the data generated and how I rendered the analysis.

CHAPTER THREE

Data Analysis

It is the mark of an instructed mind to rest satisfied with the degree of precision which the nature of the subject permits and not seek an exactness where only an approximation of the truth is possible.

Aristotle cited in Stroup, 1997, p. 125.

Foundry Context

The foundry is the most dramatic stage of the production process at Delta Technologies. There is a blend of primal and modern technologies at play. Watching molten aluminum pour from a long-handled ladle reminded me of days of antiquity marked by the metal that early humans learned to forge: the Iron Age, the Bronze Age, etc. A similar social structure of learning likely existed in those ancient communities of practice as they passed on and perfected their foundry techniques. For instance, Wenger, McDermott, and Snyder (2002) suggest:

> Communities of practice are not a new idea. They were our first knowledge-based social structure, back when we lived in caves and gathered around the fire to discuss strategies for cornering prey, the shape of arrowheads, or which roots were edible. In ancient Rome, "corporations" of metalworkers, potters, masons, and other craftsmen had both a social aspect (members worshipped common deities and celebrated holidays together) and a business function (training apprentices and spreading innovation). (p. 5)

The first thing that strikes you when you step into the foundry is that the central part of the floor is covered with sand to protect the floor from the rare spill. If the molten aluminum drips on the concrete floor, it sets off miniature explosions and cracks the floor. The liquid metal finds and expands those negligible cracks imperceptible to human eye. Because of the molten aluminum operative performance in the foundry is critical; any gaffe from standard operating procedures may be hazardous. It is not surprising that the foundry is in a separate room within the larger shop. This enclosure is designed for safety and insurance reasons. Molten aluminum could produce a catastrophe if an accident occurred; a serious error in the foundry could be lethal.

Heavy gloves and coats and boots are worn for protection when pours are performed. The working temperature of the molten aluminum is approximately 1400° F. On cold winter days the ambient temperature makes the foundry comfortably warm; on warm summer days, the foundry can be stifling. The sound of the furnace, a hollow noise of propane rushing to combust, is loud enough to make it difficult to hear conversations in the foundry. Workers need to speak into each others' ears or yell to be heard.

Lined along the walls and shelves of the foundry are patterns from previous pours. For most jobs, the foundry is the focal location of the shop since all work to this point is focused on getting a solid pour accomplished. If a pour is successful, machining and assembly is, for the most part, elemental. If the pour does not work, problems must be discovered, which may lead back through the pattern production process. By and large, success in foundry is the moment of truth for the work of the Pattern Shop.

Once the patterns are deemed ready for the foundry, after innumerable inspections, the trip to the foundry is only steps away. Using the mold as a pattern, a mixture of sand and resin is used to form a cavity for the pour. This exact sand and resin mixture is a result of a mixing tool that measures the precise amount of resin for certain moisture content of the sand. Before the mixing tool was acquired and installed, the foundry practice had problems with the quality and consistency of pours. Stories were told of the owner working late into the night attempting to get an acceptable pour completed. Now a bad pour is more the exception than the rule, but problems still arise unrelated to the sand mixture. For example, the shape of the mold can lead to not filling (or drafting) into the entire cavity.

A defective pour is a costly mistake. The aluminum can be recycled but the quality of the aluminum is degraded and is not reused in the furnace. The costs to fire up the propane furnace to melt aluminum, as well as the labor to "ram" molds in preparation for the pour, make this stage costly if the casting does not come out. When a casting does not work out, the workers tap into their learning and experience to ensure that the next pour is successful. When a pour goes awry, it is common to have the most experienced cadre in the shop circle the culprit casting and ascertain the malfunction. The collective wisdom of the shop converges to find and fix the problem. A community of practice is engaged to perfect their craft.

Introduction

Following the theme that each chapter of this research would mirror the pattern of production at Delta Technologies, the foundry has some similarity with data analysis of this research project. Similar to a pour of liquid metal, there is a fluid moment for the researcher to observe an event and render an interpretation and explanation of the events just witnessed and experienced. Using this analogy of foundry practices and analysis of data is more than a literary device to carry meaning and to convey an experience; experience (life-world) is exceedingly more complicated than a literary device can represent. Wenger (1990) puts it this way:

> Any human life-world defies description. It is always more complex, more dynamically structured, more richly diverse than any description of it. And so are the individual experiences of the people living it, shaped as they are by a nexus of interrelated factors, many of them hidden from the observer. (p. 6)

However, even the limitations of the foundry analogy with descriptions of the qualitative fieldwork nonetheless share some similarities. For example, once the molten metal is poured, it becomes inert and lifeless. Likewise, when lived experiences are reduced to words on a page, these words are simply different from the actual experience, and in some respects the words and description become inert and fixed. As much as the researcher may want to represent what transpired in the field, philosophically there always will be a gap between the experience and the depiction of that experience. Even if the reader can imagine the sand underfoot and has a notion of the enveloping heat and noise of the foundry, it is still what is known as verisimilitude. It is the plausibility of the story told that evokes a sense of authenticity.

Similarly, during each interview, I hoped that the interviewees' voices would come through to explain their experience. On a few occasions, much to my horror, I interrupted trains of thoughts, which I only noticed while later listening to the taped interview. Nevertheless, this was the raw material I had to deal with in those moments never to be repeated. Each step leads to this primeval sense-making endeavor that takes the molten actions, ideas, and words and then attempts to understand them in light of the solidified transcribed words on paper and the theoretical patterns described in Chapter Two. All the work of design and pattern making are focused on the "pour" of data analysis. And during this pour, as in the foundry, there is possibility of people being hurt by carelessness. The promise and boundaries of confidentiality could be broken inadvertently by being too specific with details, and molten thoughts shared in confidence could burn and disfigure. It is with great concern that I weld these ideas. Moreover, will the theoretical patterns hold after hours of observations and hours of interviews followed by the transcriptions of those interviews? The short answer is yes, with some qualification. The pages that follow will elaborate on this affirmation and elucidate on the qualifications.

The goals of this chapter are as follows. I will explore in detail the answers to the original research questions in Chapter One, in light of the literature review in Chapter Two and data analysis in this chapter. To reiterate, those questions were: 1) What is the organizational culture of Delta Technologies? 2) How do the participants of this organization appear to learn?

The organizational culture of Delta Technologies is exemplified in the values and assumptions evidenced in the emergent themes to follow. Technically Delta Technologies could be categorized as a meritocracy, where individuals with expertise wield the most power (see Mintzberg, 1983, pp. 388-419). Because of the complex nature of the work, few individuals are fully competent in all aspects of the production process. In order to increase the skill level throughout the organization's personnel, learning is a central concern at Delta Technologies. The bulk of the learning, however, occurs informally in contrast to the organization's explicit goals to formalize learning into written standardized curriculum. Learning would be likely enhanced if the learning systems at Delta Technologies took into account and valued the informal and social nature of how information is shared. I turn now to explain the particulars of the data analysis.

Coding

Miles and Huberman (1994) posit that "coding is analysis" (p.56), and I would add that coding is also interpretative. Simply put, coding is the means to assign "units of meaning to the description or inferential information complied during a study" (Miles & Huberman, 1994, p. 56) Another way to understand coding is that main ideas expressed in the data are summarized into chunks. The coding process occurs when the researcher analyzes large volumes of data such as field notes and interview transcriptions and puts them into manageable segments. To assist in the coding of the data, NUD*IST Vivo software was use in the management and sorting of transcriptions.

The coding methodology selected for this particular study incorporates the two main research questions (organizational culture and learning). The coding scheme is described as a blending of an inductive, context-sensitive scheme with a content-specific scheme. In other words, the specific focus of describing the organizational culture and the ways members of that organization learn was the prospective goal, combined with an inductive approach to explore how the research questions would be answered. Combining the two approaches, content-specific (learning) and context-sensitive (the organization's culture) reflect the focus of the study and the extent theory of this research topic.

Salient Themes

Six emergent themes appeared salient to me because they contain answers that address both questions about the organizational culture and the dynamics around learning. Put another way, the organizational values appear to intersect at these themes and shed light on values that both help and hinder learning and change. The themes are: 1) distinct social groups; 2) the use of humor; 3) coping with stress; 4) the bucket of rocks thing; 5) social learning revisited; and 6) metaphors.

Distinct Social Groups

The wider context in which Delta Technologies is located certainly shapes some of the nuances of its organizational culture. There is an interplay of influence between residents of the community who largely make up the personnel and the organizational culture that has emerged to serve clients such as Apple Computer and Hewlett-Packard. What I observed in this former "timber town" in the Pacific Northwest was a social and economic way of life giving way to the new information-based economy taking hold. The economic and cultural shifts, as well as some incongruities and ambiguities, were exemplified one moment early on during my observations.

A large, portly man with a bushy beard and red suspenders was shaking his head with a self-correcting sense of admonishment after an encounter with another employee. He shuffled his bulky, black boots in place and said, "I need to communicate better." Was this former logger learning the importance of clear communication in a high-tech manufacturing firm? Or was the above a result of a modified "Hawthorne Effect," where the mere awareness of researchers on the factory floor changes behavior to what the subjects think the researcher wants to see and hear?[6] Another plausible explanation for the behavior of this former logger is that he was being facetious. In hindsight, I am leaning more toward the last interpretation since I later came to experience this fellow's wry wit. The interpretative approach I have selected for this research will attempt to explain my interpretations as well as to mirror the ambiguity of everyday life.

First of all, the theme of tension between two distinct social groups at odds with each other emerged from the transcripts. This theme of a workplace culture with "us versus them" tensions only surfaced during interviews. My initial time during observations did not hint at any such tension. However, after reflection and more hours on site, I surmised that I simply did not see the tension that was present and that people were on their best behavior. At other times, values appeared more synchronized and harmonious, showing more cooperation than contention. Again, the ambiguity and variability of human relations defy either/or categories.

Nevertheless, the starting place for this interpretative study is the voice of those interviewed, and it is here in the transcripts that two social groups are suggested. I will call the first group "the learners." I describe the members of this group as a committed community of practitioners; some have university degrees in mechanical engineering, several have graduate degrees, and others have 20 years experience in a machine shop. Members of this group of learners may live in the area, but only a few were raised in the same small town. Members of this

---

[6] This classic case suggests that when you study a group in an organization, their actions will be likely altered by virtue of simply being studied. For more details see Eisenberg and Goodall (1993, pp. 71-72).

group are deeply committed to the organization and to advancing their competence in building custom molds.

The second group I will call "the laborers." This group sees themselves more as individuals interested in employment and not necessarily in professional competence. Those in this group prefer tasks that require less thinking. Learning new skills is not a priority for laborers. They work overtime when they need extra money and commitment to the firm is minimal.

Consider, for example, the tension mentioned between two social groups at Delta Technologies when Lyle (a pseudonym for a composite character) expresses his judgment and frustration.

> Well I saw... there were a lot of people that either didn't want to learn or weren't getting to learn enough, it was one or the other. There were a lot of people there that were just happy to [be] pounding vents when I were there, when I was there, and we needed people that could do more, so that I didn't have to be out fixing [mistakes].

Tom, in an interview elsewhere and at a different time, says:

> I don't mean to be stereotypical because it's probably true everywhere, but [the town where Delta Technologies is] has a mentality of that education [sic] isn't really a great thing. You know, all those people in [the college town 15 miles away], you know, those are college people. Uh, some of the guys there called me college boy, you know. It's like, well, I'm not the one with the most education here. There's a lot of people here with more [education] than me. So what? It doesn't really matter, but they, uh, they don't value education; they don't value learning opportunities. I think a lot of it is just leftover mill mentality; I go to the mill; I work at the mill; I work for the green change, the drying kiln, and eventually I'm gonna get a pension and my kid's gonna work there too. So that's what they want, that's the mentality that a lot of them have. That's really tough to live with, in any capacity.

> **Tom** continues:
> We would go on local foundry tours, far out foundry tours, mold shops, uh, anything, you know, anyplace like that that we could, because all those things contributed to our ability to solve

problems. There were other people that we would take along and try to expose to that and they didn't get it. It's like, well, why am I here, you know, this is kind of neat because we don't have to work, you know, and they thought of it as that.

Tony - A little field trip?

Tom - Right, as opposed to, oh you're working harder now. This is neck-up work and you know, it really depends on what level you're talking about, but very important for the key people to do; not so important for the other people, just because they didn't know how to convert that information into something that they could do. You know, they didn't six months down the road, say, hey, remember that shop we were in, you know, here's how they solved this problem, remember that, let's tweak that, lets figure out how to do that.

The tone of frustration and class distinction is evident in Tom's comments. The passages above highlight not only how some employees fail to take responsibility for their own learning, but also how Delta Technologies wishes an employee could learn. Being able to "covert that information" suggests the ability to see applications in other areas, apply knowledge to new challenges, and solve problems. There were certainly model employees who came from the local community who were excellent at learning from experience and then applying that knowledge in new areas. The tendency, however, is that learning as a way of life is not as important for individuals if the local societal structures, such as friends and family, do not explicitly value education. Additional interviews of those born into this community suggest that education was a less than salient value growing up in this community. For example, one young man born and raised in the area, who is training to be a plumber, said, "All you need to know about plumbing is payday is on Friday and shit runs downhill." This self-effacing comment minimizes gaining knowledge and experience in a trade that takes years to master. Plumbing may be a low-prestige position, but the plumbing trade requires many skills and years of experience. This young man apparently has learned that emphasizing your learning and expertise is not appropriate cultural behavior in his hometown.

Without making any class distinction, the founder and owner of Delta Technologies expresses his frustration with employees who are unwilling or unable to grasp their role in mistakes and learn from costly errors. He states:

> I think that's just a way, uh, sometimes you have to know that about a person, you have to hold that out there in front of them until they get it. They may never admit that they get it, or that they, that they're gonna respond to that stimulus, but some people never do get it. They don't understand what they're doing wrong... that sense of distancing themselves from their participation in the problem. It's so great that you can tell that they're gonna go on making those same mistakes because for whatever reason, maybe they're not capable of understanding. So they're never gonna learn and I think we end up probably having maybe one person like that a year that comes through here and you know. Hopefully we're getting better at recognizing that in people, but um, boy, some people just can't get it, can't understand the work we do and can't understand how to, you know, how their actions are responsible or how they're responsible for the part they played in the problem.

It was remarkable that the tension and frustration expressed in the statements above were not explicit during my months of participant observation. In fact, there was very little evidence of hard feelings and frustration until the interviews started. I remarked to a visiting trainer that the camaraderie seemed exceptional in this organization. He concurred and mentioned that he rarely sees an organization with such a positive work environment. Humor was clearly valued and played a major role in alleviating stress and tension.

The Use of Humor

Humor at Delta Technologies, although at times coarse, rarely appeared mean or vindictive. As one employee who was only there for a few months said about humor:

> ...it was allowed and people accepted it because for one, it did relieve the stress, uh, it was an easy way to deal with things and not like, you know, throw a tantrum, um, but also because it was

kind of a family you knew. I mean you knew you were joking so if somebody did say something that, you know, you wouldn't want somebody that didn't know you say, it was kind of allowed, or you joke back with them. I mean if there was ever cross the line, you know, if you just really, you know, don't say that, he'd say it in a serious tone and everybody would realize it, but there was a lot of joking around, I mean there was pretty much a bunch of brothers. (Simon)

Simon's description is pregnant with meaning. "A bunch of brothers" is indicative that the majority of employees at Delta Technologies were male. I also saw generally positive, even jovial, relations in my months on the shop floor. It seemed that humor was frequently used to relieve stress. However, it was surprising that humor used as stress relief rarely went over the line and become malicious in an industrious and competitive environment. It is noteworthy that humor is part of the "Guiding Values" in the staff handbook, where it states, "We are committed to humor." Humor is a social lubricant that helps employees working under the stress of production deadlines.

During a management training meeting, the visiting trainer remarked that the current production manager, who was in the room, was "a consummate professional." The interviews I conducted indicated that every interviewee considered this production manager extremely fair and well respected. At the same, he had intensity in his gaze that was as intimidating as a blowtorch in your face. It was immediately after the trainer praised this production manager's professionalism that a pattern maker and designer whom I learned later had had his fair share of conflicts with several people in the shop, said, " Just wait until you piss him off and see how professional he is!" There were gales of laughter in the room. Most everyone in that room had been toe to toe with that production manager and felt the heat of his words and glare. This moment of levity served to bind members in the common experience of having being "chewed out." As intimidating as this production manager could be, it was common to see staff banter with him. Wolf (2002) suggests that humor serves to share common experiences and thereby promote "normativity of the community."

Another example of joking around illustrates the limits of acceptable humor. One afternoon I was behind the foundry watching an employee clean a casting. Those in the foundry did not know I was within hearing range. One employee (yelling) remarked, "What kind of f—king operation is this?" The second employee (yelling back) replied, "Hey watch your f—king language!" I could recognize the employee's voices and the first employee was mortified when I later remarked about his joking. His unease with my inside knowledge suggested that the "Hawthorne Effect" was indeed affecting most behaviors I observed. This coarse facetiousness relieves pressure and stress; at the same time, it could have its drawbacks if those with sensitive dispositions were to find the language offensive. Be that as it may, the use of humor is an active social value within the organizational culture of Delta Technologies, as indicated in the staff handbook and in the daily practices of the staff. Besides relieving stress, humor can facilitate creativity and learning by looking at work problems in a new light.

Coping with Stress

It is not coincidental that highly specialized toolmakers of packaging or bike helmet molds use humor as a tool to cope with stress. Similar to a grinder in the hands of skilled craftsperson, humor is applied with aplomb to tension-filled situations so that the stress is kept to a manageable level. It is remarkable that humor does not become laced with frustration and anger as pressure and fatigue blur discretion. During the early participant observations, I never recorded or observed any suggestion or obvious signs of stress, such as individuals appearing tense, rushed, or on edge. People appeared busy, but not harried. Yet the ubiquitous theme of stress surfaced during the interview process with surprising frequency. Of course, the fact that I never recorded or observed stressful behavior, might be a reflection of my limitations as an ethnographer. I only saw one person being chewed out (in private), but there were stories (organizational legends) of people being dressed down in front of a large group.

As might be expected, the wide array of experience of stress suggests that some participants thrive on stress, in the same way that lifting weights strengthens a muscle. Others find the pressure counter-productive and debilitating. The atmosphere of this custom mold shop was construed in any number of ways, to the point that I wondered if people were experiencing the same workplace. As an old Hindu adage says, "We don't see the world as it is, but we see the world as we are." The interpretative emphasis of this research will attempt to take these diverse experiences and find themes that some participants share.

For all the diversity of experience, one theme that participants likely would agree upon is that stress is a major factor of work life at Delta Technologies. How people deal with the stress is a matter of temperament and volition. Tom, who by most accounts thrived under the pressure, remarked that he "would put on my game face in the parking lot." This suggests a competitive intensity that requires a persona or mask to win at a game by not showing weakness or equivocation. A hyper-competitive personality would seem to excel within Delta Technologies' culture. Consider, for instance, as Tom explains:

> The working environment is stressful. It's really hard on a lot of people, a lot of people don't have a good mechanism for dealing with that. They don't, they aren't equipped to learn, uh, about themselves personally, they aren't equipped to learn how to deal with something professionally, so they end up internalizing all that stress and don't do well there. Uh, even if you present that to them, you present ways to learn that, and a lot of them don't even know what to do with that knowledge, you know, they, it's the [small town] mentality. I think you get it everywhere, that somehow you're saying that I have a weakness and that weakness you could exploit, so I'm gonna hide it, and then take all this stress. You're not gonna know I have it, and even if you offer them tools, they see that as an opening to their weakness, so understanding and addressing that and trying to break that up, I think is an important piece [of the organizational environment].

Essentially, the culture of Delta Technologies appears to demand that employees fit the existing organizational culture rather than the culture accommodate different personality types. The first guiding value in the staff handbook reads, "We are committed to supporting the individual to ensure the success of the team." This indicates a symbiosis, where support and success are conditional upon each other. In other words, support of the individual is important if that individual "ensures the success of the team." However, what if that individual does not ensure the success of the team? The conditional aspect of this statement may not be the connotation that was desired, but some of those interviewed espoused this mutuality value, and some had left with hard feelings indicating that a social contract had been violated. For example, consider this exchange of ideas during my interview with Lyle:

> **Tony-** I'm talking more about if there was a problem you could go to [managers] whoever, and say...
>
> **Lyle-** That's right up there with my stress, I think they believed that I had a lot of the skills to just go figure it out, and sometimes I ran into that a lot of times. [The managers would say] You know, it's great that you're asking me, but I don't have the time right now, you can figure it out, we know you can, so it wasn't like just go away and leave me alone, it was like you have the abilities, now leave me alone.
>
> **Tony-** We believe in you, go away?
>
> **Lyle-** Or I don't know if it was we believe in you or we know you have the abilities, now go away. To me there's a difference.

Here Lyle expressed a subtle difference in the feeling of support from management. As the interviewer I attempted to mirror Lyle's comment, and he corrected me and made a distinction from an affirmation (not "we believe in you") to a mere acknowledgement of skills ("we know you have the abilities"). From his experience, Lyle felt that support for questions or advice in the competitive atmosphere was in short supply. In either case, these exchanges suggest that "support of the individual" may be an espoused value and not always an active value (Argyris & Schön, 1978).

This discrepancy between what the organization says formally in their mission statement and how leaders behave on the shop floor suggests an untapped source of learning. Consider how this interview continues:

> **Tony-** Um, but what I'm getting at if there were serious organizational problems that you had to concern with, [it] sound like it's very short answers, do this you'll be fine... What I'm getting at, [is that a] learning organization has the ability to change its future to what it wants to be, you know, this whole structure... this isn't working, we can change this and be a better organization for it.
>
> **Lyle-**I don't think there was a whole, yes and no, there was some openness, but at the same time there were a lot of closed ideas to the learning. Uh, and some of it came back and (the owner) was always saying um, look "outside the box, we don't ever wanta [say], this is the way we do it and this is the way we've always done it." But I guarantee you, at least once a day, I heard, "This is the way we do it; this is the way we've always done it."

Without an openness to reflect and acknowledge the discrepancy between what is officially espoused and what is practiced, learning and knowledge transfer will be hampered. Along with learning being less than optimal, there are intangibles such as interpersonal trust and a sense of community and teamwork are lost. In Delta Technologies' particular situation, it appears that the main culprit driving this integrity-deficit dynamic is stress. The major theme of this stress is the emphasis on production, to get things done and ship products to customers. Tom tells a story about a collogue within Delta Technologies who would get so agitated that Tom would take him outside and walk around the building until this collogue could calm down. With more than a few individuals indicating that stress is an issue, the next reasonable inference is that stress is a symptom or is somehow related to the active values in the organizational culture. It is noteworthy that stress is not merely a factor where individuals need to find a better coping strategy. There is a necessity to see individuals as part of a whole, each affecting the other.

The Bucket of Rocks Story

Jeremy, another employee who left and who was quite disgruntled, said the pressure to work overtime was intense. This pressure was corroborated with nearly everyone I interviewed. Working weekends and late during the week was expected if production deadlines were pending. This pressure squeezed those with children and other family concerns. One employee on the shop floor said that when he first started, he worked late every evening and on weekends until he got burned out. When there is work, managers will give you all you can handle, and sometimes more than you can handle. The overload and subsequent pressure and stress is exemplified in the bucket of rocks story that I heard in the context of being swamped with responsibility. The original story, according to Tom, is as follows:

> This guy was teaching in a Navy SEAL school and, uh, one of the things they do is they jump in an Olympic pool [with] a five gallon bucket of rocks... and swim, carrying the rocks to the other side...[Well] this guy jumped in and walked on the bottom of the pool from one end to the other and got out and whoever it was said, "Son, why didn't you swim? And [he]said, "Sir, I can't swim, sir. And [he] said, well, f--k if you'll do that, we'll teach you to swim."

Tom related this story in the context of an eagerness to learn. He goes on to say that people have misconstrued the story and diluted its "true meaning" because they are not close to the center of learning. The original "moral of the story" was transformed from one to illustrate a "Gung Ho!" attitude (Tom told me that Blanchard and Bowles, (1998) was passed around and read by leaders) to explain the sense of unfairness some employees felt, especially when someone was trying his utmost. Rather than illustrate the exceptionally ardent learner who will do anything s/he is told to do, the story is transformed to reflect the feelings of those who are "drowning in the pool and (they) throw him a bucket of rocks or tie weights on his legs." The retelling and changing of the story intimates the collective feelings of some still working at Delta Technologies. The image of a person drowning and being thrown a bucket of rocks (i.e., tasks beyond his abilities) was relayed to me on numerous occasions, with one certain person in mind. It was the impression of several employees that this person was not being treated fairly in his role as project manager.

What I find fascinating is not that the original story evolved, but how the community has changed the story to make sense of their experience. The evolution of this story is a window into the informal elements of the organizational culture of Delta Technologies. One particular project manager and the story became a negative example of what other employees did not want to emulate. Several people left the firm or stayed in production roles to avoid the stress and humiliation of taking on more responsibility. One fellow at Delta Technologies for five years recounted the enthusiasm he once had and that he now saw in newer hires. The pressure, the stress, the overtime, the reprimands "ass chewing" were not worth the effort to advance, according to this employee with five years experience. The retelling of the bucket of rocks story provides a window into some informal organizational values that have dampened an eagerness to attempt new challenges. For organizational story telling to promote learning, the story needs to reflect positive experiences of the community.

The important point here is not any one interpretation of the bucket of rocks story, but the dynamic way members of the community have reinterpreted the story to make sense of their experiences. Those with less power still have the agency to reinterpret and retell stories among themselves.

Social Learning Revisited

Learning is intertwined with the organizational culture. When social learning is considered in this context, it becomes evident that what is taught is not the lesson that is learned. People learn to hide weakness in a stressful and severe environment. Even though Tom attempted to present some ways to deal with the stress defensiveness is learned. Within the social learning paradigm there is a living curriculum, implicit and powerful, that is written by the active values of that community. Participants learn from the situation what is important, what is acceptable, and what is valued. If there are inconsistencies or contradictory values, people will interpret the "lessons" in any combination of ways.

Wenger's (1998) theory of social learning questions the assumptions about behavioral and cognitive perspectives on learning, namely, that the focus of learning is on individuals and the transfer of information. Instead, Wenger suggests that learning occurs during a complementary interplay of participation and reification. The term participation refers to the common usage of mutual engagement of a social activity. In terms of a work environment, participation is such that people bring their identities to engage in a given endeavor. Participation instills mutuality. The shared experience involves and forms the identity of those who participate. For instance, consider a young man who is learning how to work in the foundry at Delta Technologies. The daily participation of heating up the furnace, setting up the pours, donning the protective gear, and ladling in the molten aluminum gradually forms that young man's identity. After daily participation, a personal identity gradually forms in combination with that participation (for more detail, see Wenger, 1998, pp. 55-57).

Along with participation is the concept of reification. This abstract term is how participation is understood within a practice. Reification occurs when an abstraction is considered as an actual object to understand an invisible dynamic. For example, Freud (1856-1939) developed his inter-psychic theory using ego, super-ego, and id. These concepts suggested dynamics that are understood and explained with properties as if they were actual objects. Likewise, in the foundry at Delta Technologies, there is concern with whether the cavity will draft, meaning that each pocket of the cavity is filled with molten aluminum. It is not known if the cavity has drafted until the pour has cooled. Such reifications become "points of focus" (Wenger, 1998, p. 58) to understand the practice.

As practitioners participate and negotiate how these reifications pertain to the task at hand, meaning emerges in the negotiation process. Identity of participants continues, and the practice is learned and advanced. Both participation and reification work simultaneously, or at least balance each other out; one without the other will limit how learning occurs. Participation is the action; reification is the explanation.

Tom, whose parents were both professional educators, alludes to the importance of social participation. In the context of discussing experiential learning, Tom remarks, "The group that is [most] directly involved learns the best; the group that is involved with those people versus the second best and then the farther and farther you get away from it." The insight of learning as social participation came from Tom's reflection on the particular practice at Delta Technologies. He saw that the "best learning" occurs shoulder to shoulder.

Social participation is in line with the method of learning in an apprenticeship model. The training model at Delta Technologies, however, does not appear to keep participation and reification closely linked. A great deal of effort, for instance, has gone into writing "task analyses" at Delta Technologies, also known as reification. I asked a worker in the pattern shop, who had been there more than two years, where the task analyses were in the pattern shop. "Gosh," he said, "I couldn't tell you. I've never seen them." It appears that efforts to make the methods of learning certain tasks explicit through documentation were collecting dust. The curriculum was reduced to the essentials, while at the same time the living quality of that knowledge was incongruous with the effort to design task analysis.

During my interview with Tom, we touched on a similar theme. The time spent writing task analyses must be weighted against how often that information is being retrieved and used.

> **Tony**-And it's very difficult to take the intricacies of that information and document it, put it down, because this is so time consuming.
> **Tom**-Right, and unless you can train somebody in the guild manner or the apprentice manner, you really can't get that. It, uh, the apprenticeship program idea is probably the best way to go to train them there, uh, just because you really give people some idea of where they are, you give them some milestones... If you were learning to ski, you'd try to move on and do harder and harder runs. You'd try to do more, but if you don't pay attention to that, you really don't know, uh, whether or not you're doing any better. All the runs were totally unmarked, you could probably tell one was steeper than another, but if you had never been around it much, you might not notice that too much, you know.

Tom saw the value of the "apprentice manner" of training, as well as some general standard so that the learner can see some progression in their competence. Delta Technologies' training emphasis seems is geared more toward documenting the training progression, and not necessarily on actually learning the practice. This emphasis is partly due to the fact that Delta Technologies received a grant from the state to enhance their workplace training. In an effort to document and justify the training grant, time was used to corroborate this training effort. Ironically, producing the documentation appeared to be the emphasis instead of learning. For instance, another employee, I'll call Lyle spoke in an exasperated tone:

> I was also doing a lot of writing... training manuals if you go back and read a lot of those, you'll find that they're written at a pretty heady level. That's because I was, I got my... degree and I'm writing things for guys from [this small timber town], but it reads more like a major instructional manual. So I did a lot of that as well and that's where I started realizing that I was missing out on, um, I was documenting a learning process, but I wasn't living a learning process. (Lyle, emphasis with his tone of voice)

Unfortunately, Lyle eventually left Delta Technologies with his knowledge of the production process and love of learning. It is important not to allow unintended consequences attempting show that you are learning to hijack an emphasis on actual learning. The latter is akin to pulling up plants to make sure the root system is growing. Learning is more an organically occurring process; it happens through social participation while engaging in given practice. Attempting to capture the learning processes into a knowledge base is, according to Brown and Duguid (2000a), a balancing act. When communities of practitioners, not merely separate individuals, codify knowledge, the community finds a balance between knowing more than we can say (Nonaka & Takeuchi, 1995; Polyani, 1966) and explaining what we know.

Moreover, humans learn knowledge much more effectively from each other by a process known as "knosmosis" than by consulting an expert system database. This is exemplified in the following story:

> A major oil company wanted to develop an expert system that would scan aerial photographs of landscapes to locate the most promising sites to drill for oil. The company hired a leading knowledge engineer to develop the system. He spent many months working with the company's top photo analyzer, a man who proved himself extremely skilled at identifying potential drilling sites from aerial photographs. By asking the photo analyzer to provide detailed explanations of the analytic process that led to each prediction, the knowledge engineer attempted to capture the analyzer's expertise in rules that could then be expressed in a form the computer could apply. Of course, the attempt was a failure. The expert system that was produced did not even come close the degree of expertise of the human. By the end of the project, however, the knowledge engineer had himself become highly skilled at analyzing aerial photographs to predict likely drilling sites. Indeed, it was generally acknowledged that after the company's own photo analyzer, the knowledge engineer was the second-most-skilled person in the world at performing the task!
> The attempt to capture the photo analyzer's expertise in a computer system was unsuccessful, [however] the process of interacting with the analyzer to try to codify his knowledge did result in the knowledge engineer achieving a high level of expertise. In effect,

> the process of observing the photo analyzer at close range provided the knowledge engineer with an apprenticeship in geological photo analysis, a modern-day version of the traditional system whereby craftsmen of times gone by passed on their knowledge and skill to the next generation... It was a very human process of observing and interacting with the photo analyzer that led to the knowledge transfer - knosmosis. (Devlin, 1999, pp. 162-163)

Social participation at Delta Technologies is how most employees learn. The reified curriculum is stored in training modules on computer databases. There are also task analyses available for certain tasks in loose-leaf notebooks. However, during my observations I never heard an employee refer to such a notebook, and when I asked if I could see one, an employee with two year's experience said, "Gosh, I don't know where to find it." This was a thoughtful, well-educated person who functioned at very a responsible level. In other words, learning by participation, though barely recognized, was pervasive, whereas the reified curriculum, the official mode of learning, was scarcely used. The interplay between participation and reification is where meaning and personal knowledge takes shape within the reflective practitioner, which in turn helps to shape the identity of that same practitioner. Next, we turn to what metaphors may teach us about learning and the culture at Delta Technologies.

Metaphors

While the use of metaphor in interpretative organizational analysis is widely espoused and accepted (Feldman, 1991; Grant & Oswick, 1996; Lakoff & Johnson, 1980; Morgan, 1986), there are certainly limitations and disadvantages to the use of metaphors in organizational research. For instance, metaphors are recognized as ambiguous; in fact, ambiguity is actually one metaphorical theme that sheds insights into organizational dynamics (Feldman, 1991). At the same time, an interpretative approach using metaphors is one more arrow in an organizational research quiver. Researchers who see organizational research more from a scientific approach rather than a humanities approach are quick to criticize the fact that metaphors lack precision (Beer, 1981; Boulding,1987; Bourgeois & Pinder, 1983), or create so-called deleterious reifications (Tinker, 1986). With the awareness of these criticisms, Feldman's (1991) study of ambiguity as a metaphorical theme in the U.S. Department of Energy explains the value of metaphors in understanding an organization's culture:

> The meaning of ambiguity is not the same as the ambiguity itself. The meaning may vary from person to person and from setting to setting. People may, for instance, find ambiguity exhilarating or they may find it depressing. They may think of it as an unnecessary or necessary evil or as an essential and beneficial feature of their work environment. The meaning of ambiguity for any individual is complex and influenced by historical, biographical, and sociological factors. To the extent that reactions to ambiguity are common among members of the organization, the interpretation may indicate a collective understanding about ambiguity and its effects. This collective understanding is a part of the culture of that organization. (p.146)

It is this collective understanding that I wish to explore in this section. In each key interview, metaphors emerged during the data generation, such as videotaping or interviews. In some cases, I asked each respondent before I conducted the interview for a metaphor that would describe Delta Technologies or their experience at Delta Technologies.

Keeping with my interpretative theme and philosophical assumptions, I reject the notion that any metaphor or interpretation of a metaphor should be portrayed as scientific, but rather that it becomes a window into how members of an organization interpret or make sense (Weick, 1995) of their experience. The danger with any metaphor is that those ideas will become static and ossified, and accepted as definitive. Where metaphors can best be used is to think in new ways and to question the status quo, to provoke reflection on thinking. Metaphors were never intended to correspond with sociological categories; a metaphor is a literary device to suggest similarity and differences of metaphorical imagery. Chia (1996) argues that the power of metaphor is the ability to see the metaphor of metaphors. The term this use "metaphorization" and suggests:

> From this line of argument, the purpose of using metaphors in organizational analysis is not so much about whether organizations are better understood as 'machines', 'culture' or 'psychic prisons' (Morgan, 1986), but about relaxing the boundaries of thought. Nor is it about generating a rich plethora of alternative ways of viewing organizational situations; rather it is about a slow and stratified deconstructing of deeply entrenched and therefore "taken-for-granted" mode of ordering, concepts, categories and priorities, all of which collectively work to circumscribe the outer limits of contemporary managerial discourse. Conceiving of the use of metaphors as part of this process of metaphorization removes these outer limits and is therefore essential to the cultivation of intellectual entrepreneurship and the managerial imagination. (pp. 130-131)

"Relaxing the boundaries of thought" may be insightful for management to catch a glimpse of how members of an organization actually see the organization.

One way to explain the insights of organizational metaphors is by using another metaphor as an illustration. The behaviors, artifacts, documents, and so on are those aspects of culture that can be seen, like the tip of an iceberg. The larger unseen aspects of culture, which is the magnitude and the bulk of what drives the visual elements, such as assumptions, values, beliefs, may be partially understood through metaphor.

Using an iceberg model (see figure A) to explain metaphors in an organizational sense alludes to the idea that unseen assumptions and values connected to surface descriptions can yield a rich, interpretative source for "sense making." These interpreted aspects of explicit metaphors can provide a glimpse of equivocality and dissonance when compared with metaphors from other organizational members who articulate contrary values. Contradictory organizational values reveal an unraveling of the social fabric and a fracturing of the social relations by which learning and information flows within communities of practice. If there were a more authentic meeting of the minds, knowledge and learning would become more evident.

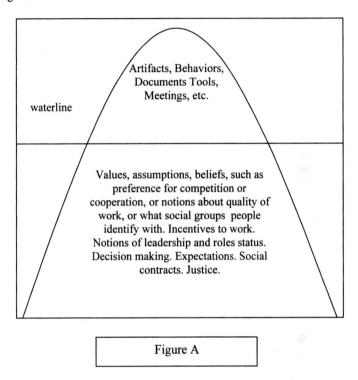

waterline

Artifacts, Behaviors, Documents Tools, Meetings, etc.

Values, assumptions, beliefs, such as preference for competition or cooperation, or notions about quality of work, or what social groups people identify with. Incentives to work. Notions of leadership and roles status. Decision making. Expectations. Social contracts. Justice.

Figure A

Metaphors expressed by those who worked at Delta Technologies range from shocking imagery to the more mundane, pedestrian metaphors. What is remarkable is that the metaphor question was mentioned prior to some interviews, so respondents had some days to ponder their metaphor(s) of choice. Certain metaphors were used repeatedly, so I believe these comments were not off-the-cuff, flippant remarks, but reflected a deep-seated impression toward what is valued by organizational participants and how they interpreted their reality. Similarly, the metaphors and values espoused by the owner were recorded on video during a new employee orientation, which would suggest that this orientation was thoughtfully and purposely chosen. Nevertheless, when the various metaphors are compared, as might be expected, incongruities abound. These experiences of reality are akin to the description of the group of blind men describing an elephant. Rather than coming to some point where a complete pachyderm can be on display for inspection, discontinuities and contradictions will be highlighted to suggest where fault lines have fractured feedback loops. Further reflection might create greater openness to learning and increase social cohesion if organizational defensiveness could be minimized.

The first and rather predictable metaphor for a small firm is that of an extended family, replete with distant relatives that annoy some members. Stories about the early days of the firm, having dinner around the table saw, working until two in morning, driving to Portland all night to deliver a set of molds that were promised, all suggest a bonding that can sometimes connect people closer than family members. As Chris puts it:

> ...there are a few individuals out there like that and then you have your, you know, your favorite cousins or whatever, nephews, nieces, people you goof around with, brothers, have great fun with... I think there are even a few figures that could sort of, could fill the capacity of an elderly family member that, um, people get annoyed with and take them for granted, maybe, and that, well, they're just old and senile. What do they know? You know, they're kind of a pain in the ass... there are people out there that maybe would be the same role as an annoying brother-in-law or stupid cousin... Every now and then you just wanta beat the hell out of them...they keep doing the same stupid things over and over and never learn.

Both positive and negative elements of belonging to a clan were mentioned in this elaboration of a family. The expressions of annoyance were not evident during my observations on the shop floor. The consistently cordial behavior could partially be attributed to the Hawthorne Effect and management's admonitions to act professionally; upon reflection, it seems that employees were on their best behavior for this research. In addition, while I was studying Delta Technologies, the company was at one of the high points in its hiring and production history (approximately 65 employees). The above quote suggests that some workers were kept on, even though their performance was found lacking, because of the abundance of work. Unfortunately, after several months of layoff and sporadic weeks of work here and there, more than a few skilled and valuable employees found employment elsewhere. There was not enough work at Delta Technologies to keep them employed, and they could not live on unemployment payments and an infrequent work schedule. When the economy weakened and there were extensive layoffs, only a very few employees remained on the payroll. Management might call those remaining the most skilled or most loyal employees. I should mention that Chris's remarks were made during a boom time. When the economy weakened and people were laid off, some employees were less generous when other employees were still at work.

This acrimony was exemplified by an employee who has since left with some very hard feelings about the particularism (a term he did not use) that he saw toward certain employees, i.e., the way the owner showed some employees favoritism. With an organization that has the history of a "mom and pop" establishment that grew into a multi-million dollar operation, showing a particular preference for those who had been with the owners from the beginning, through good and bad times, is easy to understand. However, at the same time, this situational issue eventually will need to be addressed for the firm to navigate its future direction and will be considered in the next chapter. The remainder of this chapter will highlight the theme of uneven relationships, or particularism, which appears exaggerated in light of what appears to be a difference between espoused values and active values.

The Sphere or Global Metaphor

It is easy to conjecture why the owner, a sculptor with a Master in Fine Arts degree and environmental concerns selected a sphere or a global metaphor to represent of the organizational structure at Delta Technologies. Three-dimensional shapes have been part of the owner's life for a long time, both as a sculptor and mold maker. The idea that positions on a sphere suggests equality and lack of hierarchy. One expression of this value is the fact that business cards at Delta Technologies do not have titles.

While the notion of equality is espoused as an explicit company value, interviews with employees suggest that these equality values are ideals that are not always practiced. Several respondents, one still employed, displayed a cynical smirk when I brought up the owner's global metaphor of organizational equality during interviews. One employee replied:

> [The owner is] very into global philosophy and global community, um, and I, you know, metaphorically, it's global, but each one of the parts of the shop represents the different stage of a country; you have third world countries in that job, ok, so there are not, there is not that sense of equality, there is a third world.

The difference between the actual and the ideal resulted in other employees feeling disillusioned and betrayed before they left. One reason for the gap between these espoused values and actual values appears to be that other values take precedence. The words of the owner during a new employee orientation, tends to be the most operative value: "Do whatever it takes to get products out the door." This economic bottom line is on the mind of nearly every small business owner. The pressure to keep the doors open is hard to fully empathize with unless you have been close to that pressure, as I was with my father's small business. Thus, writing this analysis is not intended to portray any simplistic good and bad characters. Rather, I hope to show how remarkably different our experiences can be. If we can begin to see those differences not as right and wrong, but simply as different, then we may learn different perspectives and become more aware of the collective experience at Delta Technologies.

While learning is considered to be a competitive advantage in business (Stata, 1989), time must be "spent" toward learning to add value. One theme I saw repeatedly was the hurry to get products out the door. Consider, for example what Larry said:

> I'm not quite sure how to put this, they [Delta Technologies] are extremely interested in keeping up with current techniques and materials and procedures for a cost effectiveness basis [sic]. But often times, uh, we're so busy out there that it's very difficult to take the time to go through the trial and error learning curve to implement new techniques and materials... we sort of get stuck in this rut of doing the way we know how because that's the way we can get it out the door.

During the new employee orientation, the owner made the claim that work takes on a life of its own; the work becomes the boss. This claim appears to take power out of the owner and employees' hands and to place the power in some impersonal work order and deadlines. When pressed, the owner agreed that work is negotiated and that the sales office and customer agree to "the work" and a certain deadline. However, the owner responded that if the "most experienced employees were doing the work, we could finish this mold well under budget and before the deadline." What the owner says may be true, but he misses the point of how to raise the level of competence of employees. Products are getting out the door, but employees who cannot handle the stress walk out the door as well. By emphasizing production, learning is conflated with the production process and becomes one more thing to produce, such as a task analysis, a training report or manual, as if learning and knowledge is merely something to quantify and produce. Similar to an organization, learning perhaps is conceived better as process, not a product, as a verb and not a noun (Hall & Paradice, in press). Accepting that learning is a social process suggests that social context constitutes the actual lessons that are learned. Those at Delta Technologies have expressed implicitly the social nature of learning in an often-quoted phrase that was posted in the design shop: "Telling is not training." It could be added that "information transfer is not learning." Learning involves of the totality of a person embedded in social network, so that specialized (tacit) knowledge is imparted during social participation in a practice (Wenger, 1998). If that social context is laden with stress and tension, then incongruities or alternative issues to cope with that stress diminish learning and practice.

The next two metaphors depict why the context might be considered as stressful. Tom said that if mentioning his name would help improve Delta Technologies, it would be fine to use it. However, I decided to keep all names fictitious for the sake of consistency, and yet, in this case, to leave in enough detail in so those insiders could deduce "Tom's" identity so that credibility could be ascribed to his comments. Tom was considered a star that would never leave Delta Technologies. He also was resented by some whom I interviewed as the owner's "golden child" who could do no wrong. In that respect, he epitomized someone who would succeed at Delta Technologies.

> **Tony-** Remember I mentioned in that e-mail about a metaphor. Do you have a metaphor that you'd use for Delta Technologies?
> **Tom-**Uh, I did think about this, but its, uh, I like cars, Delta Technologies' kind of a, Delta Technologies is a handful. If you've ever been around sports cars or even like bicycles or skis or anything, there are some that are really easy to drive, you know, that are Cadillacs, you get in and they're cushy and everything is just so, but really they just go kind of in a straight line. Delta Technologies wants to be a sports car but they haven't really refined it yet, you know, so it's a handful to drive, you gotta be on all the time, uh, it uh, it's kind of twitchy, it's kind of finicky, you gotta tune it, you gotta do things to it all the time and you're always working on it, it's uh, it's a perpetual deal, you don't just go to work there, it's, when you drive up to the shop, you put your game face on as you drive up to the shop, you are uh, you're getting ready to go in. I used to have just a mental image of I would walk in and put on this heavy rubber coat so that the blood wouldn't get on me, you know, yeah, and every day as I drove up, that's what I would do and every night, I'd take it off mentally and hang it at the door and try to make it so that when I got home, I wasn't worried about it any more.
>
> **Tony-**Tell me more about this, you know, the blood flying... body parts, you know, that's the image I'm getting,
> **Tom-**Yeah, it was very stressful, it was very stressful for me to work there, um, I don't know that everybody feels a lot of stress, it

uh, I did a lot of different things, uh, you know, would meet with very high level customers, would make a lot of decisions on molds and stuff before they would ship on how they would be done, uh, just all kinds of stuff, you know, that, uh, I realize there were other people there who had equal or more stress than I did.

The imagery and experience conveyed by Tom in his sports car metaphor is corroborated by and consistent with other parts of his interview. Both the exhilaration and stress of his rapid rise into leadership indicates the multiple segments of Delta Technologies' organizational culture. The excitement and thrill of driving a sports car, along with high maintenance to keep the car running, alludes to Tom's hobby of amateur car racing.

The second depiction is striking for its evocative imagery. The protective nature of the metaphors "put on your game face" and "rubber coat and boots" is remarkable because Tom indicates that these imaginary protective devices were used as daily coping mechanisms so as to not to be soiled by the "blood." An additional remark about the global metaphor fits here as well, although it did not come from Tom. Another employee I will call Sal that said you have to remember that "liquid hot magma [is] in the middle," to indicate the passion present at Delta Technologies just below the cool surface. The sports car metaphor seems to suggest the risk and fun that Tom clearly experienced, whereas the slaughterhouse allusion depicts the messy, stressful daily experiences. The latter image is about protection from the stress; the former is thriving on the stress and excitement. Each metaphor focuses on the positive and the negative aspects of stress, separate sides of the same coin.

However, when stress becomes more salient, it does not merely affect the individual, but also the relationships between the individuals- the collective whole. How do Tom's metaphors fit his performance, which suggest that he was an exemplary employee (his rapid rise to leadership) and his pejorative unofficial nickname (the owner's golden child), in light of what the owner asserts: "Delta Technologies' culture is how we treat each other, with respect and dignity"?

Using an imaginary protective metaphor does not preclude treating each other with respect and dignity. However, it does suggest that the work situation is seething with stress, so that some feel the need for protection.

The value that seems to lead to this stress is "to do whatever it takes to get products out the door." It appears that short-term profitability (or maybe survival) is sought, rather than long-term sustainability. This theme of sustainability will be considered in next chapter.

Before I conclude this section, I want to consider one last metaphor used by the owner- a type of metaphor not used by anyone else at Delta Technologies. The context of the next statement was related to "knowledge reserve" from the organizational learning profile instrument: "Is the knowledge in a database or in personnel?" The answer was that it was mainly in its people:

> ... One of the reasons that our training program has taken so long to develop is because it's, you know, how do you suck that information out of somebody and what is in words, um, yeah, I'd say most of that lies within the personal side.

I recognize that metaphor here is a casual figure of speech, but knowledge, especially tacit knowledge, is not something you can vacuum or pump out of someone. With the recognition that metaphorical analysis has its limits, metaphors indicate how we construe the world around us. Metaphors are tools for understanding our mode of interpretation, reflections of how we understand the world. It is not surprising that those at Delta Technologies who make metal tools with other tools might think in mechanical ways, as opposed to organic metaphors such as gardening. Perhaps looking at knowledge development as a naturally occurring process might benefit Delta Technologies with more a sustaining and nurturing perspective rather than a mechanical metaphor.

The implications and applications of these data will be discussed in the next chapter.

CHAPTER FOUR

Discussion and Conclusion

Adults do not set out to become fearful, but most are encouraged at some time in their life to be certain. The sense of security that comes from certainty is more addicting than opium. We all want to be right. However, unless adults finally realize and admit that they cannot be and are not certain of anything and that they have been fearful of many things (including living and loving and learning), that childlike sense of hope and awe and passion for life cannot return. Conversely, when that realization and admission do take place the paralysis of fear and certainty abates and the power to act returns.

Maybe fear and certainty use up all the free energy necessary for action, and it seems to me that creativity can only become manifest through action. A humble openness to and acceptance of uncertainty drives out fear. All of the creative role models I have ever known or admired were humble men and women of faith and action.

Larry McFarlane, MD

Assembly Context

The Assembly Department is the final stage of the production process at Delta Technologies. Once an acceptable aluminum casting emerges from the foundry and lands in the Assembly Department, the most difficult work already has been done. The hours spent in design, pattern making, and the foundry, however have yet to produce an actual tool. The Assembly Department is the stage of the work process during which precise parts are trimmed off the casting and miscellaneous parts are assembled to make a tool according to the customer's specifications.

The Assembly Department is where most new employees start on production work. It is at this stage of production where a new employee can see the finished product and the sum total of the production process. The assembly stage is labor intensive and the work can be tedious. Details, precision, and fit are all necessary to finish a functional tool. Delta Technologies has an industry-wide reputation for building quality molds. To ensure the high standards of quality, checks and double checks each step of the way ensure that measurements fall within a prescribed level of tolerance.

While some tasks such as drilling vent holes and pounding vent inserts are repetitious and require minimal skill, other tasks such as running a computerized machining drill press that cuts exact patterns require specialized skills and training. The level of precision can be as exact as 1/100 of a millimeter. Mistakes at this point of the production process are usually fixable (rather than starting over with a new casting), but most mistakes cut into profits because of the hours spent repairing the mistake. The loss in profit increases if the customer discovers the error and Delta Technologies must pay the round trip shipping costs. Fortunately for Delta Technologies' bottom line, the latter type of mistake is rare.

What is not rare in the assembly department, however, is the wide array of noise produced. Most of the ambient noise generated on the shop floor comes from the Assembly Department. The noise does not seem out of the ordinary until someone starts pounding away on a mold with a ball peen hammer or a grinder rips into a casting and yellow- red metal sparks fly into shifting, spraying patterns as the grinding wheel shaves off the unwanted metal. After standing in this department for several hours, it is clear why ear protection is recommended.

Assembly is also a busy location. Projects that arrive behind schedule to Assembly Department still have the same deadline to ship. Those in the Assembly Department are ready to point this actuality out whenever deadlines are brought up. The shipping date is looming and the pressure is on to meet the deadline. Customers who order these custom molds must have the mold completed correctly and on time so that they can, in turn, fill their customer's orders. An entire line of printers or computer components could be delayed if a package mold is not done right and on time. The pressure to finish and ship molds on time can make Assembly a hectic, stressful place.

Project managers (PMs) mingle in the Assembly area to answer any questions and monitor progress or problems. More than any other department, Assembly inspects and re-inspects specifications before signing off. However, even with all the inspections, problems occasionally slip through the production process. For instance, the issue of mirroring is a consistent source of potential problems. When making a mold, in the exact opposite shape, numbers, or insignia must also be factored in so that the finished tool will produce what the customer specified. With all the thousands of measurements and points to check, it is still notoriously easy to overlook the most obvious points. Attention to detail and a reliance on collective learning is evident, since a different set of eyes might catch what was missed previously. There is collective learning based on the memory of lessons learned from past glitches.

An example where the organizational memory reflects the culture at Delta Technologies is evident in the way humor is used. Near the back door there is very small aluminum tombstone with SAE RIP. SAE stands for "Society of Automotive Engineers" that standardized American wrench and bolt sizes such as ½" or ⅝" (as opposed to the metric system). Leaders at Delta Technologies prefer the metric system because it gives more precise measurements, especially when dealing with exact machining cuts. At one point, both systems were used, which caused endless headaches when drill bits and bolts were mixed up; there are enough details to keep track of without using two different sets of measurements.

The Assembly Department takes up the most floor space in the production process. Space is needed to assemble, machine, vent, clean, and weld all the parts of a custom mold into large sheets of thick aluminum plate. The finished mold tools can be as large as a king-sized bed, with copper pipe cooling systems. More space and the large machinery, such as a forklift, are needed to package and load finished custom molds onto trucks.

The tasks of the Assembly Department, more than during any other stage of production, are driven by the exact specifications of the customer. In essence, Delta Technologies is a custom mold shop that makes tools for bicycle helmet manufacturers and other more generic manufacturers to make packaging foam to safely ship their products. In each case, the safety of the bicycle rider or the protection of products during shipping is ultimate reason for production of these custom mold tools. The Assembly Department is the final production stage of assemblage that makes these parts into a workable tool.

Introduction

In the pages that follow, I will suggest how insights gleaned during this ethnographic inquiry might enhance the organizational learning and learning climate at Delta Technologies, thereby promoting a long-term growth trajectory for the company. It is my hope that the leadership at Delta Technologies will seriously consider the descriptions and quotations. There are those who hold that "constructive criticism" is an oxymoron. However, most writers, for example, recognize the value of a critical eye before presenting their work to a wider audience. Whatever uncomfortable insights were divulged, I suggest that the feelings and comments offered by current and past employees are voices from which learning can take place, and to ignore or dismiss troubling comments will merely perpetuate the same climate. Argyis (1992) suggested that organizational defensiveness blocks learning from mistakes. Be that as it may, I trust the prognosis will be more palatable than the diagnosis.

Discussion

To understand the learning climate at Delta Technologies, it may prove helpful to consider a concept called social capital. Portes (1998) traces the origins of social capital to French sociologist Pierre Bourdieu (1985). The value of social relationships in a business environment, and a less academic explanation, is found in Cohen and Prusak (2001). Social capital shares some similarities with terminology such as intellectual capital or human capital, in an attempt to account for capital expenditures on a balance sheet. Cohen and Prusak's definition is as follows: "Social capital consists of the stock of active connections among people: the trust, mutual understanding, and shared values and behaviors that bind the members of human networks and communities and make cooperative action possible" (p. 4).

Social capital has an illusive, intangible quality that pertains to the "group chemistry" and how a group gets along. Organizations can still succeed with low social capital, but at a price. And organizations with high social capital still can fail. Social capital is not a substitute for quality products or services, marketing, or strategy. Organizations are tremendously complex, and they operate in complicated markets and environments. Social capital is merely an important ingredient in the mix for communities of practice and learning to flourish.

There also may be danger and disadvantage when social capital becomes exclusive and trust exists only within the inside group. The group's focus is narrowed and ultimately diminished with an unconstrained loyalty for the group and its ideas and ideas or opinions from outside are suspect. Some religious groups take on this tendency, but so can any social group that thinks of itself as exclusive. Groups that have exceptionally strong social capital can become impervious to new ideas because new ideas may challenge "the way we have always done it."

From my observations, at least at the beginning of the fieldwork, Delta Technologies displayed a positive, thriving social capital. On the surface, people clearly cooperated with each other, and they produced some remarkable work together. The coordination and technical expertise in the production chain appeared relatively smooth and seamless --all well oiled by mutual respect. But as with any organization or cluster of social relationship, conflicts and discontinuities exist below the surface. It is no surprise that disharmony is present at Delta Technologies. What surprised me was that the tension was so well concealed during months of observation; and the first hint of disharmony surfaced during confidential interviews.

It is not that the productive quality of relationships at Delta Technologies is extraordinarily deleterious. It is not. Delta Technologies is one of the more harmonious and productive workplaces I have observed. In some respects, it seems perplexing that such strong notions about the debilitating stress and tension surfaced during interviews. The longer I spent time on the shop floor, the more I was trusted with the unvarnished opinion of employees and learned that the quality of relationships could be much more conducive to learning. I interviewed several who had left Delta Technologies; were quite bitter and disillusioned with their experience of feeling marginalized and undervalued. It seems wise, in light of the relatively high turnover rate, (approximately 70% in the life of the organization) to consider the reasons each person chose to leave Delta Technologies. Each of these broken relationships, not only the few I interviewed, represents a series of mistakes that have cost Delta Technologies thousands of dollars in labor cost, in the hours spent by both the trainee and by the trainer. During the new employee orientations that I taped, the owner and founder suggested the absurdity of not being explicit in explaining when a mistake occurs so that learning may take place. Might we compare personnel failures to aluminum castings that must be thrown out and recycled? From my experience on the shop floor I saw an acute concern when aluminum castings did not work out. I believe if dozens of aluminum castings (at over $1000 apiece) were tossed out, management would make it a top priority to find out why and fix the problem. And yet the cost of employee turnover is many times the cost of an aluminum casting.

From my experience at my father's firm and as a maintenance supervisor, I concede that finding and retaining competent, responsible employees is a challenge. One expects some to wash out, some to move on simply because they are younger and want new career opportunities, some because of other personal reasons, and some for a combination of reasons. However, several I interviewed at Delta Technologies remarked (and I summarize here) that it was the gap between what management said and how management acted that led to their resignation. One complained vociferously of an arbitrary, informal pay schedule. When I conducted the research there was not standardized pay schedule (to the best of my knowledge), such as after one year and acquisition of a certain skill set, the hourly wage would be X. Others said that suggestions or requests were dismissed on a regular basis.

Empowerment is a buzzword that is often tossed around. In some cases, bright, assertive people are allowed to run with projects, almost to the point of being on their own without much support or advice. Others are given authority, but with arbitrary limits on what they could do. In either case, not having guidance or a clear understanding of one's limits can magnify work-related stress (Mikkelsen, Saksvik, & Ursin, 1998). Moreover, a few employees said they heard two contradictory messages — one that said explicitly, "You're empowered," and another message that implied that empowerment was limited to the work in front of you, and that larger processes or policy decisions were not your concern. This experience of "surplus powerlessness" (Lerner, 1986) is certainly not limited to Delta Technologies, yet is epitomized in an event I videotaped. What precipitated this event and the event itself would have likely have been missed if I only relied on observation, because it transpired in just seconds. The videotape allowed me to watch repeatedly how the frustration quietly builds. The following description is purposefully opaque so as not to reveal the identity of the participants.

The meeting I refer to was a department quality meeting (known as DQUAL). Each participant represented a department and was given the title of Quality Assurance Manager for his/her department. The owner was not present at this meeting. It was a warm Friday afternoon and the meeting was scheduled to end at the end of the workday. Participants appeared tired from a week of work. Discussion went around and around over an idea to provide a drawing of a proposed design so the pattern shop would have a ballpark idea about what to build. The merit and cost of drawings was discussed for at least a half-hour. It became evident that the group, without the owner present, had no authority to make this decision. After a long pregnant pause, a key person facetiously asked the person who made the original proposal, " How about you send me an e-mail?" At that moment, a third person tossed an empty paper water cup in exasperation and jest at the person who asked for the e-mail. Nervous laughter percolated throughout the room, evidently relating to standard operating procedure of how "empowerment" works at Delta Technologies. At a later time, another person who had been in the room revealed in a two-hour interview the frustration of documenting quality issues or production ideas, only to see those ideas "die in some database" because someone close to the owner nixed the idea.

At another DQUAL meeting someone spoke of "the powers that be," as if Delta Technologies was a large, cumbersome bureaucracy rather than a small, agile high-tech manufacturing firm of 50 individuals. It seems that power is concentrated in the select few who have the owner's ear. The ramifications of such an informal power structure appears debilitating to learning; employees are told they have a voice and equal standing in the firm, (such as equal status on a sphere) when in actuality the equality is mainly contingent on truly outstanding performance. As a result of putting non-articulated conditions onto values, it should not come as a surprise that employees feel marginalized and feel little sense of responsibility, as social contracts appear invalidated. As Dr. Scott Simmerman (1998), a management consultant, has said, " No one ever washes a rental car." In other words, people behave in direct proportion to their sense of responsibility when they feel a sense of ownership.

Even if the owner does not want to share ownership, such as developing and offering stock options, at the very least there must be greater integrity between what is espoused and what is practiced. No relationship can thrive if trust does not exist between the parties. To declare egalitarian values on one hand and then practice privilege on meritorious performance of a few is simply detrimental to social learning and social capital. It would be more actuate to describe Delta Technologies as a collaborative meritocracy (Mintzberg, 1983, pp. 388-419), with a robust core group (Kleiner, 2003). Congruence between espoused values and active values are no small matter. Cohen and Prusak (2001) put it more forcefully:

> Nor is social capital demonstrated or enhanced by lip service to equity and respect. Calling everyone in an organization an "associate" [or manager] when in fact most have no decision-making power or direct participation in the organization's success merely breeds cynicism. Since social capital is about trust, relationship, and commitment, it thrives on authenticity. Hypocrisy kills it. (p.14)

Social learning theory argues that learning is situated and for learning to occur the learning context is as significant as the curriculum. If people (or employees) in that context do not feel they are legitimate participants in the community of practice then competency and responsibility will prove thin. The greatest asset of Delta Technologies is not the hard capital such as property and machinery, but rather the skills and intelligence of employees and the fine reputation it has gained from its customers because of the high quality of work those employees produce.

The summarizing claim of this research, and that of social learning theory, is that for learning to take place, four factors must be considered as mutually constitutive, all interacting simultaneously. First, the learning process shapes the identity of the learner. Second, the meaning of experience is constructed in the learning process. Third, engagement in practice or activity with participation is fundamental to social learning. Some activities and individual proclivities are more suitable to learning alone; however it is rare for activities or individuals to not reengage socially at some point, once a task or skill is learned. Fourth, belonging is rudimentary to learning and having a sense of legitimization within the community engaged in a given practice. Communities of practice emerge and form spontaneously because learning is a social process. Perhaps what Delta Technologies can do is to understand how these four elements are expressed on their shop floor, cultivate professional camaraderie, and remove defensive routines that may hinder learning. Below are some specific suggestions.

Suggestions

Structurally Delta Technologies appears to be in a quandary between an entrepreneurship and a professionally managed firm. Delta Technologies seems to be professionally managed at first glance but upon closer scrutiny an arbitrary discretion is retained, exemplified, for instance, in the lack of a standard pay schedule. The founder makes most important decisions (with the input of few close, long-time friends who also work there; the core group). If Delta Technologies wants to become a professionally managed firm, the owner will need eventually to formalize the management systems. If the owner wishes to retain personal control, Delta Technologies could remain a small custom mold shop and be quite successful. However, the transition from an entrepreneurship to a professionally managed firm is an issue outside the scope and range of this dissertation, but should be considered for the health and future of Delta Technologies (see Flamholtz, 2000, for a helpful introduction on how to manage this transition). The future structure of Delta Technologies is important; any suggestions acted upon should take into account what sort of organizational structure is planned and projected.

Delta Technologies appears to be a victim of its own success. Its ability to churn out quality custom molds on time and near budget is remarkable. This custom mold shop market niche is to respond to orders as the manufacturing sector is going through upheavals. Delta Technologies has grown and contracted as the manufacturing sector has gone through irregularities in economic pattern. Most investment advisors would suggest that diversification and planning is crucial for long-term success. If Delta Technologies could develop some other means of cash flow that would allow for their trained work force to stay productive when custom mold orders slow, the work force could remain employed; a production machine shop is not the only alternative. Using in-house expertise and generating other businesses to provide another revenue stream could be explored. This is where some fresh thinking is needed, and possible business scenarios with start-up costs would need to be considered. Planning is a form of learning (de Geus, 1997) and as the saying goes: Those who fail to plan, plan to fail.

Further, the management needs to be even more selective of employees who are hired. One suggestion for finding new employees or apprentices is to check with local high school shop teachers for bright seniors with a strong work ethic and mechanical aptitude. New employees need to be thought of as apprentices and long-term colleagues. New employees could know that they might be selected to become apprentices. Those who are not selected as apprentices remain part of the general labor force and do not receive the shoulder-to-shoulder training unless they distinguish themselves. If new employees catch show promise, a position might be offered to them with a benefit that helps them attend engineering classes at one of the local universities. If formal school is not the desire of these apprentices and they still show an aptitude toward learning the craft mold making, they could still move on to learn pattern making, machining, foundry work, and eventually, design work.

Another method of improving employee (new hires) selection is to hire a psychology graduate part-time to administer personality tests. Again, diversity of personality types is normally more advantageous for new insights to emerge. Valuing different strengths allows people to understand, appreciate, and get along with others. Common wisdom suggests that homogeneity weakens the community dynamics. It is important to remember that communities of practice cannot be planned, controlled, or even managed. They emerge spontaneously because people share an interest in a given practice. At best, communities of practice may be cultivated and encouraged rather than designed and manufactured (Wenger et al. 2002).

Providing more activities that allow for informal meetings and sharing some food together is something that Delta Technologies does quite well. I suggest that this practice be advanced even more to promote camaraderie. For example, there was a chili cook-off during my fieldwork; it was a great example of how community "happens," and similar events could be regularized into the yearly calendar. Another way Delta Technologies shows appreciation to its people and encourages community is when birthdays are recognized with a cake. Giving people positive feelings while they are at work is money well spent. Good tasting food and time together to enjoy it will likely help generate feelings of appreciation (see Creating Community Anywhere, by Shaffer and Anundsen, 1993, for more ideas).

A local hospital offers "Mindfulness Based Stress Reduction" training that might prove helpful to employees feeling overwhelmed. This eight-week workshop originates from Jon Kabat-Zinn (1990) at the University of Massachusetts Medical Center and provides simple, yet profound, techniques to reduce stress. While this workshop may prove useful to some, Delta Technologies also needs to be more aware of how the workload and tight deadlines may overextend employees and their families. Workplace stress, from my perspective, should be dealt with at both the situational and the personal level, not one or the other.

While moderate amounts of stress at work are normal and even healthy, similar to physical exercise, there is a pernicious form of stress that emerges from silencing conflict. Stress emerges here from a passive, defensive realization that denying what one thinks is a more welcomed than honesty. This internalized stress must be swallowed because of the fear of loosing one's job. It is the social or organizational norm that prescribes and values compliance over honesty. Wenger (1998) argues the identity of the apprentice is shaped by social experience of the learning context. As the learner is asked to silence their authentic voice, their identity is squelched and truncated. Perlow found that silencing conflict hindered learning and innovation in the organization she studied (2003, pp. 42-51). Delta Technologies would increase its propensity to learn if they understood the subtle patterns that promoted reticence over expression in their firm.

Lastly, to reiterate, the organization should work toward integrating what is espoused and what is practiced. To some degree the gap between professed values and active values seems endemic to every organization with which I have been in contact. The healthiest and most vibrant organizations are the ones that face this gap with candor and treat this information as an impetus for organizational learning.

Study Limitations and Suggestions for Further Research

This interpretative, inductive, and ethnographic study has attempted to explore textures of organizational life inaccessible by quantitative methods. The limitation of this portrait is specific to the context of Delta Technologies in the particular time frame of the fieldwork. A dramatic slowdown in the United States economy (also known as the dot-com bubble bursting) started roughly at the same time as this research. The slowdown in the greater manufacturing sector also affected the tone and mood of Delta Technologies. When work slowed down and most employees were laid off for weeks a time, Delta Technologies clearly was changed. Several employees looked for and found work elsewhere, but as even employees were asked back and as work became available, the social dynamic was altered.

The particular details and context of this study are also the study's limitations. The strength of this story comes from details embedded in the particular situation. Any transferability would depend on the degree of similarity between the two contexts.

Further research could take several directions. Compiling "learning histories" of Delta Technologies might help promote a more reflective community (Senge et al., 1999). This time consuming method of research would document lessons learned from past experiences. This method of research requires that employees do the bulk of writing; an editor and researcher then work with the parties involved to compile a readable, useful document of organizational folklore that portrays lessons learned.

A second study could examine another custom mold shop in another part of the United States to compare the two firms. If Delta Technologies were to grant permission, one could develop an in-depth questionnaire, and ramifications raised in this quantitative study could be explored. At the very least, Delta Technologies would benefit if anonymous employee feedback was solicited on a monthly basis. Without protection of anonymity, most firms will not hear employees' unvarnished opinions. Frankly, most employees need their jobs too much to be honest. However, by understanding what employees think, as shocking as it may sound to management personnel, a firm can move past mere compliance to a partnership where learning is a way of life.

About the Author

Anthony M. Barrett is a first generation college graduate. He received his A.B. in Anthropology (with a minor in Linguistics) from San Diego State University. He then earned his M.A. in Cross-Cultural Studies from Fuller Theological Seminary. He completed his Ph.D. in Education, with an emphasis in Adult and Organizational Learning from the University of Idaho. He currently resides in northern Idaho with his wife and daughter and works as a learning consultant. He can be contacted at ambarrett@adelphia.net .

Bibliography

Ackoff, R. L. (1994). *The democratic corporation: A radical prescription for recreating corporate America and rediscovering success.* New York: Oxford University Press.

Argyris, C. (1957). *Personality and organization.* New York: Harper Collins.

Argyris, C. (1962). *Interpersonal competence and organizational effectiveness.* Homewood, IL: Dorsey Press.

Argyris, C. (1964). *Integrating the individual and the organization.* New York: Wiley.

Argyris, C. (1965). *Organization and innovation.* Homewood, IL: R. D. Irwin.

Argyris, C. (1970) *Intervention theory and method: A behavioral science view.* Reading, MA: Addison Wesley.

Argyris, C. (1980). *Inner contradictions of rigorous research.* New York: Academic Press.

Argyris, C. (1985) *Action science, concepts, methods, and skills for research and intervention.* San Francisco: Jossey-Bass.

Argyris, C. (1990). *Overcoming organizational defenses: Facilitating organizational learning.* Boston: Allyn and Bacon.

Argyris, C. (1992). *On organizational learning.* Cambridge, MA: Blackwell.

Argyris, C., & Schön, D. (1978). *Organizational learning: A theory of action perspective.* Reading, MA: Addison-Wesley.

Argyris, C., & Schön, D. (1996). *Organizational learning II: Theory, method and practice.* Reading, MA: Addison-Wesley.

Armon, C. (1993). Developmental conception of good work: A longitudinal study. In J. Demick and P. Miller (Eds.), *Development in the workplace* (pp. 21-37). Hillsdale, NJ: Lawrence Erlbaum Associates.

122

Atkinson, P., & Hammersley, M. (1994). Ethnography and participant observation. In N.K. Denzin & Y. S. Lincoln (Eds.), *Handbook of qualitative research* (pp. 248-261). Thousand Oaks, CA: Sage Publications.

Bandura, A. (1977). *Social learning theory.* Englewood Cliffs, NJ: Prentice-Hall.

Bandura, A. (1986). *Social foundations of thought and action: A social cognitive theory.* Englewood Cliffs, NJ: Prentice Hall.

Banks, S., & Banks, A. (Eds.).(1998). *Fiction and social research: By fire or ice.* Walnut Creek, CA: AltaMira Press.

Barbour, I. (1974). *Myths, models and paradigms: A comparative study in science and religion.* New York: Harper & Row.

Bateson, G. (1972). *Steps to an ecology of mind: Collected essays in anthropology, psychiatry, evolution, and epistemology.* San Francisco: Chandler.

Beer, S. (1979). *The heart of enterprise.* New York: Wiley.

Beer, S. (1981). *Brain of the firm.* New York: Wiley.

Bell, D. (1973). *The coming of post-industrial society.* New York: Basic Books.

Berger, P. (1990). *Sacred canopy: Elements of a sociological theory of religion.* New York: Doubleday.

Berger, P., & Luckman, T. (1966). *The social construction of reality.* Garden City, NJ: Doubleday.

Bernstein, R. J. (1983). *Beyond objectivism and relativism: Science, hermeneutics, and praxis.* Philadelphia: University of Pennsylvania Press.

Blanchard, K., & Bowles, S. (1998). *Gung ho!: Turn on the people in any organization.* New York: William Morrow, Inc.

Boulding, K. E. (1956). General system theory: The skeleton of science. *Management Science, 2,* 197-208.

Boulding, K. E. (1987). The epistemology of complex systems. *European Journal of* Operational Research. 30, pp. 110-116.

Bourdieu, P. (1985). The forms of capital. In *Handbook of Theory and Research for the Sociology of Education.* (ed.) Richardson , J. G. pp. 241-58. New York: Greenwood.

Bourgeois, V.W., & Pinder C.C. (1983). Contrasting philosophical perspectives in administrative science: A reply to Morgan, *Administrative Science Quarterly, 28* (4), 608-613.

Bowker, G. C., & Star, S. L. (1999). *Sorting things out : Classification and its consequences.* Cambridge, MA: MIT Press.

Bridges, W. (1991). *Managing transitions: Making the most of change.* Reading, MA: Perseus Books.

Brindle, M., & Stearns, P. N. (2001). *Facing up to management faddism: A New look at an old force.* Westport CT: Greenwood Publishing Group.

Brown, J.S., Collins, A. & Duguid, P. (1989). Situated cognition and the culture of learning. *Educational Research, 18* (1), 32-42.

Brown, J.S., & Duguid, P. (1991). Organizational learning and communities of practice: Toward a unified view of working, learning and innovation. *Organization Science, 2,* 40-57.

Brown, J. S., & Duguid, P. (2000a May-June). Balancing act: How to capture knowledge without killing it. *Harvard Business Review,* 73-80.

Brown, J. S., & Duguid, P. (2000b). *The social life of information.* Boston, MA: Harvard Business School Press.

Brown, J. S., & Solomon-Gray, E. (1995, November) The people are the company. *Fast Company,* 78-82.

Burns-McCoy, N. (1998). Spinning yarns: Evaluating the tales qualitative researchers tell. (Doctoral dissertation, University of Idaho, 1998).

Burr, V. (1995). *An introduction to social constructionism.* London: Routledge.

Burrell, G. (1996). Normal science, paradigms, metaphors, discourses and genealogies of analysis. In S. Clegg, C. Hardy, & W. Nord (Eds.), *Handbook of organization studies* (pp. 642-658). London: Sage.

Burrell, G. & Morgan, G. (1979). *Sociological paradigms and organizational analysis.* London: Heinemann.

Carr, A. (1997). The learning organization: New lessons/thinking for the management of change and management development? *Journal of Management Development, 16* (4) 224-232.

Carr, W., & Kemmis, S. (1983). *Becoming critical: Education, knowledge and action research.* Victoria, Australia: Deakin University Press.

Chia, R. (1996). Metaphors and metaphorization in organizational analysis: Thinking beyond the thinkable. In D. Grant & C. Oswick (Eds.) *Metaphor and Organizations.* (pp.127-145). London: Sage Publication.

Cohen, D., & Prusak, L. (2001). *In good company: How social capital makes organizations work.* Boston, MA: Harvard Business School Press.

Coles, R. E. (1999). *Managing quality fads: How American business learned to play the quality game.* New York: Oxford University Press.

Collins, F. (1997). *Social reality.* London: Routledge.

Congressional Reports (2002) *Joint inquiry into intelligence community activities before and after the terrorist attacks of September 11, 2001* (S. Rept. 107-351). Retrieved September 5, 2003, from http://www.gpoaccess.gov/serialset/creports/911.html

Cook-Gumperz, J. (Ed.). (1986). *The social construction of literacy.* Cambridge: Cambridge University Press.

Corman, S., Banks, S., Bantz, R., & Mayer, M. (Eds.). (1990). *Foundations of organizational communication: A reader.* New York: Longman.

Corporate culture: The hard-to-change values spell success or failure. (1980, October 27). *Business Week*, pp. 148-160.

Covey, S. (1989). *Seven habits of highly effective people.* New York: Simon & Schuster.

Coy, M. (Ed.).(1989). *Apprenticeship: From theory to method and back again.* Albany, NY: State University of New York Press.

Creswell, J. W., & Miller, D. L. (2000). Determining validity in qualitative inquiry. *Theory Into Practice.* 39 (3), 124-130.

Crossan, M. M. (1999, July). An organizational learning framework: From intuition to institution. *Academy of Management Review,* 24 (3), 522-538.

Crossan, M. M. & Guatto, T. (1996) Organizational learning research profile. *Journal of Organizational Change Management,* 9 (1) 107-112.

Dawson, C. (1958). *Religion and the rise of western culture.* GardenCity, N.J.: Image Books.

Dechant, K. & Marsick, V. J. (1991). In search of the learning organization: Toward a conceptual model of collective learning. *Proceeding of the Eastern Academy of Management,* pp. 225-228. Hartford, CT.: Eastern Academy of management.

Deems, T. (1997). Vital Work: Meaning and experience within the natural workplace. (Doctoral dissertation, University of Nebraska- Lincoln, 1997).

De Geus, Arie. (1997). *The living company.* Cambridge, MA: Harvard Business School Press.

De Pree, M. (1993). *Leadership jazz.* New York: Dell.

Deming, W. E. (1986). *Out of crisis.* Cambridge, MA: MIT Center for Advanced Engineering Study.

Denzin N. K., & Johnson, J. M (1993). *The alcoholic society: Addiction and recovery of the self.* Somerset NJ: Transaction Publishing.

Denzin, N.K. & Lincoln, Y. S. (Eds.). (1994). *Handbook of qualitative research.* Thousand Oaks, CA: Sage Publications.

Devlin, K. (1999). *Infosense: Turning information into knowledge.* New York: W.H. Freeman and Company.

Dewey, J. (1933). *How we think: A restatement of the relation of reflective thinking to the educative process* (Revised ed.). Boston: D. C. Heath.

DiBella, A. J., & Nevis, E. C. (1998). *How organizations learn.* San Francisco: Jossey-Bass.

Draft, R. L., & Weick, K. E. (1984). Toward a model of organizations as interpretation systems. *Academy of Management Review.* 9 (2), 284-295.

Drucker, P. F. (1999, October). Beyond the information revolution. *The Atlantic Monthly, 284* (4), 47-57.

Easterby-Smith, M., Crossan, M., & Nicolini, D. (2000). Organizational learning: Debates past, present and future. *Journal of Management Studies. 37* (6) 783-796.

Eisenberg, E. M. & Goodall, H. L. (1993). *Organizational Communication: Balancing creativity and constraint.* New York: St. Martins Press

Ely, M., Anzul, M., Friedman, T., Garner, D., & Steinmetz, A. C. (1991). *Doing qualitative research: Circles with circles.* New York: Falmer.

Emery, F. E. (Ed.). (1969). *System thinking: Selected readings.* New York: Penguin.

Feldman, M. S. (1991). The meaning of ambiguity: Learning from stories and metaphors. In P.J. Frost, L. F. Moore, M.R. Louis, C.C. Lundberg, & J. Martin (Eds.)*Reframing organizational culture* (pp. 145-156). Newberry Park, CA: Sage Publications.

Fiol, C. M. & Lyles, M. (1985). Organizational learning. *Academy of Management Review, 10,* 803-13.

Flamholtz, E. (2000). *Growing pains: Transitioning from an entrepreneurship to a professional managed firm.* New York: Wiley (first published in 1986 as *How to make the transition from an entrepreneurship to a professional managed firm.* San Francisco: Jossey-Bass.

Foucault, M. (1977). *Discipline and punish: The birth of the prison.* New York: Pantheon Books

Frost, P.J., Moore, L.F., Louis, M.R., Lundberg, C. C., & Martin, J. (Eds.). (1991). *Reframing organizational culture.* Newberry Park, CA: Sage Publications.

Fulmer, R. M., & Keys, J. B. (1998, Autumn). A conversation with Peter Senge: New development in organizational learning. *Organizational Dynamics*, pp. 33-42.

Garrison, J. (1995). Deweyan pragmatism and epistemology of contemporary social constructivism. *American Educational Research Journal. 32* (4), 716-740.

Geertz, C. (1973). *The interpretation of cultures.* New York: Basic Books.

Geertz, C. (2000). *Available light: Anthropological reflections on philosophical topics.* Princeton, NJ: Princeton University Press

Gergen, K. J. (1994). *Realities and relationships: Soundings in social construction.* Cambridge, MA: Harvard University Press.

Goodman, N. (1978). *Ways of worldmaking.* Indianapolis, IN: Hackett.

Grant, D., & Oswick, C. (Eds.).(1996). *Metaphor and organizations.* London: Sage Publications.

Gravin, D.A. (1993, July-August). Building a learning organization. *Harvard Business Review, 7*(4), 37-46.

Greiner, L. E. (1972, July-August). Evolution and revolution as organization. *Harvard Business Review, 50* (4) 37-46.

Grondin, J. (1995). *Sources of hermeneutics.* Albany, NY: State University of NewYork Press.

Gummesson, E. (1991). *Qualitative methods in management research.* Newbury Park, CA :Sage.

Hacking, I. (1999). *The social construction of what?* Cambridge, MA: Harvard University Press.

Hall, D., & Paradice, D. (in press). Philosophical foundations for a learning-oriented knowledge management system for decision support. *Journal of Information Technology Applications.*

Handy, C. (1993) *Understanding organizations.* New York: Oxford University Press.

Hanson, N. R. (1958). *Patterns of discovery.* New York: Cambridge University Press.

Harvard Business Review. (1997, Sept.-Oct.) 75th anniversary issue. Vol. 75 (5).

Hatch, M. (1997). *Organization theory: Modern, symbolic and postmodern perspectives.* New York: Oxford University Press.

Hedberg, B. L.T. (1981) How organizations learn and unlearn, In P.C. Nystrom & W.H. Starbuck (Eds.). *Handbook of organizational design.* (Vol. 1, pp.3-27) New York: Oxford University Press..

Hewitt, J.P. (2001). The social construction of social construction. *Qualitative Sociology 24* (3), 417-423.

Heylighen, F. (1997). Occam's razor. Retrieved October 10, 2003, from http://pespmc1.vub.ac.be/OCCAMRAZ.html

Hickman, L. (2001). *Philosophical tools for technological culture: Putting pragmatism to work.* Bloomington, IN: Indiana University Press.

Hiley, D. R., Bohman, J. F., & Shusterman, R. (Eds.). (1991). *The interpretative turn: Philosophy, science, culture.* Ithaca, NY: Cornell University Press.

Huber, G. P. (1991). Organizational learning: The contributing processes and the literatures. *Organization Science, 2,* 88-115.

Husserl, E. (1970/1936). *The crisis of European science and transcendental phenomenology.* (D. Carr, trans.). Evanston, IL: Northwestern University Press.

Jelinek, M. (1979). *Institutionalizing innovation: A study of organizational learning systems.* New York: Praeger.

Kabat-Zinn, J. (1990). *Full catastrophe of living: Using the wisdom of your body and mind to face stress, pain, and illness.* New York: Dell.

Katz, D., & Kahn, R. (1978). *The social psychology of organizations.* New York: Wiley.

Kearney, M. (1984). *World view.* Novato, CA: Chandler & Sharp.

Kim, D. H. (1993, Fall). The link between individual and organizational learning. *Sloan Management Review, 35* (1) 37-50.

Kimberly, J., & Miles, R. (1980). *The organizational life-cycle: Issues in the creation, transformation, and decline of organizations.* San Francisco: Jossey-Bass.

Kleiner, A. (1996). *The age of heretics: Heroes, outlaws, and the forerunners of corporate change.* New York: Doubleday.

Kleiner, A. (2003). *Who really matters: The core group theory of power, privilege, and success.* New York: Doubleday.

Kolb, D. A. (1984) *Experiential learning: Experience as the source of learning and development.* Englewood Cliffs, NJ: Prentice-Hall.

Kuhn, T. (1970). *The structures of scientific revolutions* (2nd ed.). Chicago: University of Chicago Press.

Lakoff, G., & Johnson, M. (1980). *Metaphors we live by.* Chicago: University of ChicagoPress.

Latour, B., & Woolgar, S. (1979). *Laboratory life: The social construction of scientific facts.* Beveley Hills, CA: Sage Publications.

Lave, J., & Wenger, E. (1991). *Situated learning: Legitimate peripheral participation.* New York: Cambridge University Press.

Lerner, M. (1986). *Surplus powerlessness: The psychodynamics of everyday life and The psychology of individual and social transformation.* Oakland, CA: The Institute for Labor and Mental Health.

Levin, D., Cross, R., & Abrams, L. (2002). *Why should I trust you? Predictors of interpersonal trust in a knowledge transfer context.* Paper presented at Academy of Management, Denver, CO, August 19th.

Levitt, B., & March, J. G. (1988). Organizational learning. *Annual Review of Sociology, 14,* 319-340.

Lewin, K. (1948). *Resolving social conflicts: Selected papers on group dynamics.* New York: Harper & Row.

Lewin, K. (1951). *Field theory in social science.* New York: Harper & Row.

Lincoln, Y. S., & Guba, E.G. (1985). *Naturalistic inquiry.* Beverly Hills, CA: Sage Publications.

130

Lorber, J., & Farrell, S.A. (1991). *The social construction of gender.* Newbury Park, CA: Sage Publications.

Lubrano, A. (2004). *Limbo: Blue-collar roots white collar dreams.* Hoboken, NJ: John Wiley & Sons, Inc.

Lyotard, J.-F. (1984). *The post modern condition: A report on knowledge.* Minneapolis: University of Minnesota.

Manville, B., & Ober, J. (2003, January). Beyond empowerment: Building a company of Citizens. *Harvard Business Review,* 48-53.

March, J. G. (1991, February). Exploration and exploitation in organizational learning. *Organization Science, 2* (1), 71-87.

March, J. G. & Olsen, J.P. (1975). Organizational learning under ambiguity. *European Journal of Policy Review, 3* (2) 147-71.

McFarlane, L. (2003, July, 9). Faculty of creativity [LO30341] Message posted to Learning Organization List, archived at http://www.learning-org.com/03.07/0012.html

McGill, M. E., & Slocum Jr., J. W. (1993, Autumn). Unlearning the organization. *Organizational Dynamics, 22* (2), 67-79.

Merriam, S., & Caffarella, R. S. (1991, 1998). *Learning in adulthood: A Comprehensive guide.* San Francisco: Jossey-Bass.

Mikkelsen, A., Saksvik, P. Ø. & Ursin, H. (1998). Job stress and organizational Learning climate. *International Journal of Stress Management,* 5 (4) pp.197-209.

Miles, M. B., & Huberman, A. M. (1994). *Qualitative data analysis: A sourcebook of new methods* (2nd ed.). Thousand Oaks, CA: Sage.

Mintzberg, H. (1983). *Power in and around organizations.* Englewood Cliffs, NJ: Prentice-Hall.

Morgan, G. (1986). *Images of organization.* Newbury Park, CA: Sage.

Morgan, G., & Smircich, L. (1980). The case for qualitative research. *Academy of Management Review, 5* (4) 491-500.

Morris, E. (2000). *Dutch: A memoir of Ronald Reagan.* New York: Random House.

Nonaka, I. (1991, November- December) The knowledge-creating company. *Harvard Business Review, 69* (6) 96-104.

Nonaka, I. & Takeuchi, H. (1995). *The knowledge-creating company: How Japanese companies create the dynamics of innovation.* New York: Oxford University Press.

Oldfather, P., & West, J. (1994, November) Qualitative research as jazz. *Educational Researcher,11*, 22-25.

Orr, J. E. (1996). *Talking about machines: An ethnography of a modern job.* Ithaca, NY: ILR Press.

Oxford English Dictionary (1989). Oxford: Clarendon Press

Perlow, L.A. (2003). *When you say yes but mean no.* New York: Crown Business.

Phillips, D.C. (Ed). (2000). *Constructivism in education: Opinions and second opinions on controversial issues.* National Society for the Study of Education 99th yearbook, Vol.1. Chicago: University of Chicago Press.

Pipher, M. (1996). *The shelter of each other: Rebuilding our families.* New York: Ballantine.

Polanyi, M. (1958). *Personal knowledge: Toward a post-critical philosophy.* Chicago: University of Chicago Press.

Polkinghorne, J. (1996). *Beyond Science: The wider human context.* New York: Cambridge University Press.

Portes, A. (1998). Social capital: Its origins and application in modern society. *Annual Review of Sociology, 24* 1-24.

Potter, J. (1996). *Representing reality: Discourse, Rhetoric, and social construction.* London: Sage Publications.

Redding, J. & Catalanello, R. F. (1994). *Strategic readiness: The making of the learning organization.* San Francisco: Jossey-Bass.

Rogers, C. R. (1995). *On becoming a person: A therapist's view of psychotherapy.* Boston: Houghton Mifflin.

Rogoff, B. 1990. *Apprenticeship in thinking: Cognitive development in social context.* New York: Oxford University Press.

Rogoff, B. & Wertsch, J. (Eds.) (1984). *Children's learning in the zone of proximal development: New direction for child development.* San Francisco: Jossey-Bass.

Rorty, R. (1979). *Philosophy and the mirror of nature.* Princeton, NJ: Princeton University Press.

Rorty, R. (1999). *Philosophy and social hope.* London: Penguin.

Sandberg, J. (2000). Understanding human competence at work: An Interpretative approach. *Academy of Management Journal 43* (1), 9-25.

Sanjek, R. (Ed.). (1990). On ethnographic validity. In *Fieldnotes: The makings of anthropology.* Ithaca, NY: Cornell University Press.

Sarbin, T.R., & Kitsue, J.I. (Eds.). (1994). *Constructing the social.* Thousand Oaks, CA: Sage Publications.

Schein, E. H. (1992). *Organizational culture and leadership.* San Francisco: Jossey-Bass.

Schein, E. H. (1996, Fall). Three cultures of management: The key to organizational learning. *Sloan Management Review, 38* (1), 9-20.

Schön, D. A. (1967) *Invention and the evolution of ideas,* London: Tavistock (first published in 1963 as *Displacement of Concepts*).

Schön, D. A. (1973). *Beyond the stable state: Public and private learning in a changing society.* New York: Random House.

Schön, D. A. (1983). *The reflective practitioner: How professionals think in action.* New York: Basic Books.

Schön, D. A. (1987). *Educating the Reflective Practitioner.* San Francisco: Jossey-Bass.

Schwandt, T. A. (1994). Constructivist, interpretivist, approaches to human inquiry, in N.K. Denzin, & Y. S. Lincoln, (Eds.), *Handbook of Qualitative Research* (pp. 118-137.) Thousand Oaks, CA: Sage Publications.

Schwandt, T. A. (2001). *Dictionary of qualitative inquiry* (2nd ed.). Thousand Oaks, CA: Sage Publications.

Scott, J. (1998). *Seeing like a state*. New Haven, CT: Yale University Press.

Searle, J. (1992). *The rediscovery of the mind*. Cambridge, MA: MIT Press.

Senge, P.M. (1990). *The fifth discipline: The art and practice of the learning organization*. New York: Doubleday.

Shaffer, C. R. & Anundsen, K.(1993). *Creating community anywhere*. New York: Putnam.

Shotter, J. (1992). Getting in touch: The meta-methodology of a postmodern science of mental life. In S. Kvale (Ed.), *Psychology and postmodernism*. London: Sage Publications.

Shrivastava, P. (1983). A typology of organizational learning systems. *Journal of Management Studies 20* (2) 7-28.

Simmerman, S. (personal communication, June 1, 1998).

Simon, H. A. (1991). Bounded rationality and organization. *Organization Science, 2*(1) 125-34.

Smilkstein, R. (2003). *We're born to learn: Using the brain's natural learning process to create today's curriculum*. Thousand Oaks, CA: Corwin Press.

Smircich, L., & Calás, M. (1987). Organizational culture: A critical assessment. In F. Jablin, L. Putnam, K. Roberts, & L. Porter (Eds.), *Handbook of organizational communication* (pp. 226-263). Newbury Park, CA: Sage.

Smith, M. K. (2003a) Chris Argyris: Theories of action, double-loop learning and organizational learning. *The online encyclopedia of informal education*. Retrieved October 2, 2003, www.infed.org/thinkers/argyris.htm

Smith, M. K. (2003b). Donald Schön: Learning, reflection and change. *The online encyclopedia of informal education*. Retrieved October 2, 2003, www.infed.org/thinkers/et-Schön.htm

Smith, M.K. (2003c). Learning Theory: *The online encyclopedia of informal education*. Retrieved October 2, 2003, http://www.infed.org/biblio/b-learn.htm

Sperschneider, W., & Bagger, K. (2003). Ethnographic fieldwork under Industrial constraints. *International Journal of Human-Computer Interaction 15* (1), 41-51.

Spradley, J.P. (1980). *Participant observation*. New York: Holt, Rinehart and Winston.

Star, S. L. (1991). The sociology of the invisible: The primacy of work in the writings of Anselm Strauss. In D. R. Maines (Ed.), *Social organization and social process: Essays in the honor of Anselm Strauss*, pp. 265-283. New York: Aldine de Gruyter.

Stroup, W. F. (1997). Webs of chaos: Implication for research designs. In R. Eve, S. Horsfall, & M. E. Lee (Eds.) *Chaos, complexity, and sociology: Myths, models, and theories* (pp.125-140). Thousand Oaks, CA: Sage Publications.

Stata, R. (1989, Spring). Organizational learning: The key to management innovation. *Sloan Management Review, 30* (3) 63-74.

Stendahl, K. (1976). *Paul among Jews and Gentiles and other essays*. Philadelphia, PA: Fortress Press

Suchman L., Bloomberg, J., Orr, J. & Trigg, R. (1999). Reconstructing technology as a social practice. *American Behavioral Scientist 43* (3), 392-408.

Tarnas, R. (1991). *The passion of the western mind: Understanding the ideas that have shaped our world*. New York: Ballantine.

Taylor, F. (1913). *The principles of scientific management*. New York: Harper.

Tinker, T. (1986). Metaphor or reification: Are radical humanists really Libertarian anarchists? *Journal of Management Studies, 23*, 363-585.

Toulmin, S. (1960). *The philosophy of science: An introduction.* New York: Harper.

Vaill, P. B. (1996). *Learning as a way of being: Strategies for survival in a world of permanent white water.* San Francisco: Jossey-Bass Publishers.

von Bertalanffy, L. (1956). General system theory. *General systems: Yearbook of the society for the advancement of general systems theory.* Vol.1 pp.1-10.

von Glasersfeld, E. (1995). *Radical Constructivism: A way of knowing and learning.* London: Falmer.

Vygotsky, L. S. (1978). *Mind in society: The development of higher psychological process.* Cambridge, MA: Harvard University Press.

Wax, R. (1971). *Doing fieldwork: Warnings and advice.* Chicago: University of Chicago Press.

Walkins K. E., & Marsick, V. J. (1993). *Sculpting the learning organization: Lessons in the art and science of systemic change.* San Francisco: Jossey-Bass.

Weber, M. (1947/1924). *The theory social and economic organization.* Glencoe, IL: Free Press.

Webster's New World Dictionary (3rd ed.). (1991). New York: Prentice-Hall

Weick, K. F. (1979a). Cognitive processes in organizations. In B. M. Staw (Ed.) *Research in organizational behavior* (pp. 41-74). Greenwich, CT: JAI Press.

Weick, K. F. (1979b). *The social psychology of organizing* (2nd ed.) New York: Random House.

Weick, K. F. (1991). The nontraditional quality of organizational learning. *Organization Science, 2,* 116-24

Weick, K. F. (1995). *Sensemaking in organizations.* Thousand Oaks, CA: Sage.

Weick, K. E., & Westley, F. (1996). Organizational learning: Affirming an oxymoron. In S. Clegg, C. Hardy, W. Nord (Eds.), *The handbook of organization studies* (pp. 440-458). Beverly Hills, CA: Sage.

Wenger, E. (1987). *Artificial intelligence and tutoring systems: Computational and cognitive approaches to the communication of knowledge.* San Mateo, CA: Morgan Kaufman.

Wenger, E. (1989). Intelligent tutoring systems: Beyond expert systems. *International Journal of Applied Engineering Education, 6* (2), 279-291.

Wenger, E. (1990). Toward a theory of cultural transparency: Elements of a social discourse of the visible and the invisible. (Doctoral dissertation, University of California- Irvine, 1990).

Wenger, E. (1996). Communities of practice: The social fabric of a learning organization. *Healthcare Forum Journal, 39* (4), 20-26.

Wenger, E. (1998). *Communities of practice: Learning, meaning, and identity.* NewYork: Cambridge University Press.

Wenger, E. (personal communication, May 20, 2003).

Wenger, E., DcDermott, R., & Snyder, W. (2002). *Cultivating communities of practice.* Cambridge, MA: Harvard Business School Press.

West, C. (1989). *The American evasion of philosophy: A genealogy of pragmatism.* Madison: University of Wisconsin Press.

Whyte, W. F. (1956). *The organization man.* Garden City, NJ: Doubleday.

Wiener, N. (1961). *Cybernetics or control and communication in the animal and the machine* (2nd ed.). Cambridge, MA: MIT Press.

Winograd, T., & Flores, F. (1986). *Understanding computer and cognition: A new foundation design.* Norwood, NJ: Ablex.

Wolcott, H. F. (1990). *Writing up qualitative research.* Thousand Oaks, CA: Sage.

Wolcott, H. F. (1994). *Transforming qualitative data: Description, analysis, and interpretation.* Thousand Oaks, CA: Sage.

Wolf, M. P. (2002). A grasshopper walks into a bar: The role of humor in normativity. *Journal for the Theory of Social Behavior, 32* (3), 330-343.

Zwicky, J. (1992). *Lyric Philosophy.* Toronto: University of Toronto Press.

Index